The Essential
WILDERNESS
NAVIGATOR

The Essential
WILDERNESS
NAVIGATOR

David Seidman

Illustrations by Christine Erikson

Ragged Mountain Press
Camden, Maine

For Laura,
My compass and guiding star.

Published by Ragged Mountain Press

10 9 8 7 6 5 4 3

Library of Congress Cataloging-in-Publication Data

Seidman, David.
    The essential wilderness navigator / David Seidman : illustrations by Christine Erikson.
       p.   cm
    Includes bibliographical references (p. 155) and index.
    ISBN 0-07-056323-3
    1. Wilderness survival. 2. Orientation. I Title. II. Title: Wilderness navigator
GV200.5.S44 1995
796.5'1—dc20

95-30840
CIP

Questions regarding the content of this book should be addressed to:
Ragged Mountain Press, P.O. Box 220, Camden, ME 04843

Questions regarding the ordering of this book should be addressed to:
The McGraw-Hill Companies, Customer Service Department, P.O. Box 547, Blacklick, OH 43004
Retail customers: 1-800-822-8158, Bookstores: 1-800-722-4726

A portion of the profits from the sale of each Ragged Mountain Press book is donated to an environmental cause.

The Essential Wilderness Navigator is printed on 60-pound Renew Opaque Vellum, an acid-free paper which contains 50 percent recycled waste paper (preconsumer) and 10 percent postconsumer waste paper. ♻

Printed by Quebecor Printing, Fairfield, PA
Text design by John Reinhardt
Production and page layout by Janet Robbins
Edited by Jonathan Eaton, John Vigor
Photos on pages 72-77 by Jeff Slack, Classic Photography
Cover design by Ann Aspell
Cover: Map photo and upper left inset, Richard Procopio; lower left inset, Randy Ury

CONTENTS

ACKNOWLEDGMENTS

The manuscript for this book was reviewed by Wallace Robbins, longtime Maine forester, professor, and outdoorsman; Chris Townsend, backcountry traveler and author; and Steve Howe, writer/photographer/outdoorsman and Southwest Editor for *Backpacker* magazine. For their valuable insights and criticism, I am indebted. Any remaining inaccuracies or infelicities are mine. I also want to thank Christine Erikson for the fine illustrations she rendered from my crude sketches.

Publisher's Note

Ragged Mountain Press thanks the Brunton Company, of Riverton, Wyoming, and especially Dan Burden, for the loan of several compasses during production of this book.

Of the several fine books quoted in the pages to come, *Snow Man* is long out of print, and it seems *The Journals of Lewis and Clark* may also be out of print in 1995. *Lost on a Mountain in Maine,* an amazing nonfiction "as-told-to" account of a 12-year-old boy's several-day wilderness trial, appears to be back in print in a couple of different editions.

INTRODUCTION

This book is for all outdoorspeople, and for those who *would* be outdoorspeople were it not for the fear of getting lost. Staying found is not an instinct or an innate skill; like riding a bicycle or mastering municipal bus routes, it can be learned.

Indeed, the basics can be learned quite quickly, and most outdoorspeople are content with that. But the more time we spend outdoors, and the more adventurous we become, the greater the chances of encountering a situation that baffles our orienteering skills. It could be a trick of the weather, a few minutes' inattention, a decision to cut across country to a visible destination rather than following the trail—and suddenly panic is rising as you're forced to admit to yourself that you don't know where you are.

This book explains how to stay out of those situations, and what to do when you *do* get lost. It has been laid out in a progressive format. You start here, go to there, and then finally wind up where you want to be. Once you've learned something, you use it as a steppingstone to other knowledge. As ideas accumulate, you'll be surprised how far you've progressed. It will all be done in small doses. It will be easy to head back if you think you're not yet fully in the picture—which is how you should explore any unknown area.

Chapter 1 provides basic training for perceiving the environment. No one is born with a sixth sense. What passes for it is the learned ability to observe—to see, smell, hear, and sense details in the world you pass through. You have to learn all this, and I'll show you how. This chapter contains the most important sentence in the book: *If you*

plan to return along the same route, turn around frequently to see what your path will look like on the way back.

In Chapter 2 we'll take the next step, to learn what cannot be sensed. We'll do this with maps, which are the most effective way of portraying parts of the world beyond our vision. Of course, you could also use the written word, but think how cumbersome it would be to describe even the smallest patch of land in sufficient detail to allow strangers to find their way. If a picture is worth a thousand words, then a map is a complete guidebook. But it is a guidebook written in its own language, a language I'll show you how to interpret. Once you can do this, the world is in your hands.

Next I'll give you a point of reference that can be used anywhere on the planet, and a gadget that always shows where it is. This gadget, as you might have guessed, is a compass. It gives wayfinding insurance and, once you know its tricks, provides the ultimate in dependability. As you'll see, it is a guiding finger that does a lot more than point north.

Next, you'll put it all together. Taking your newfound sense of direction and ability to read a map and use a compass, you can start to navigate. And as you practice, you'll learn when you can relax precision for the sake of convenience and speed. You'll discover that, in practice, land navigation consists for the most part of orienting off surrounding landmarks such as distant peaks, river drainages, or slope aspects and angles. The compass is used mostly to orient the map to these landmarks, and then for rough intermediate bearings that help you field-check that you're following the appropriate "line of least resistance" in the desired direction.

As time goes by, you'll find most often that you just travel with map in hand, keeping up with passing landmarks, rather than plotting and following exact directional vectors. Vegetation, obstacles, and game trails (which can be followed quickly) will all divert you somewhat from your plotted bearings. Seldom will you stick to tight courses or make square, equal-sided detours around obstacles as this book sets forth.

But we walk before we run, and it is good to learn map-and-compass navigation as a discipline before you practice it as an art.

In Chapter 6 we move beyond map and compass use to examine some of the signs that can be found in nature. Chapter 7 touches lightly on specialized navigation for extreme environments. Neither chapter pretends to be thorough, but they show you further directions to explore.

And exploration is what this book is about.

Bon voyage!

Chapter One

A SENSE
OF DIRECTION

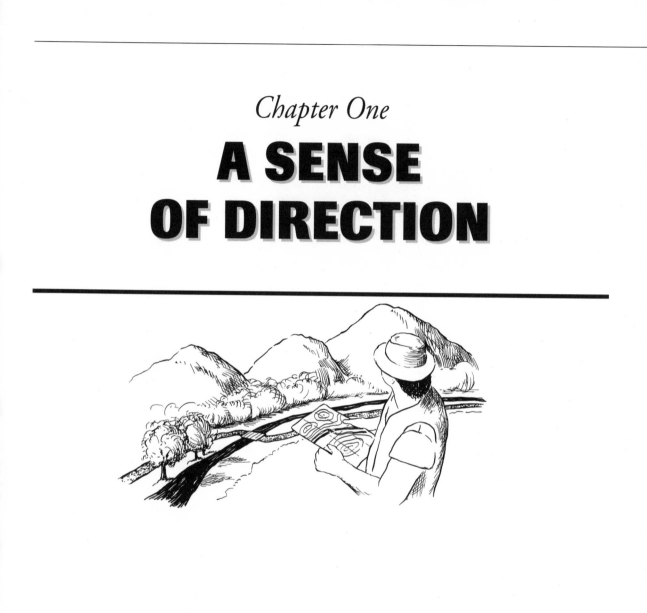

This is the most important chapter in the book, and also the most challenging. All that follows will be about specialized techniques, presented in cookbook style—straightforward methods anyone can learn. But the contents of this chapter are not so clear-cut and cannot be presented in such a direct manner.

The next few pages explore the mindset of the navigator—a way of looking at your environment and sensing the clues around you. This will help you make better use of the techniques you'll learn later, and ultimately even liberate you from them.

Primarily this chapter is about judgment, a way of bringing all your senses to bear on the bigger problem.

Good judgment is no less present in the art of getting around without getting lost—more often known as navigating—than in other fields of endeavor. Technique is fine and necessary, but it's a foundation of good, informed judgment that keeps you out of trouble.

Luckily for us, as in other fields, this judgment is not inherited. It can be learned. To become a proficient navigator you don't need the genes of a Vasco da Gama or a Daniel Boone (who claimed never to get lost, although he had on occasion been *bewildered* for several days at a time). Nor is this judgment a mystical power, such as European explorers once attributed to "primitive natives." To be sure, there seemed to be extrasensory ability involved, but it was only the hard work of people trying to survive. They were great wayfinders, but they had to practice all their lives to get that way.

To help you on your way, here's the foundation stone of all wayfinding, and the essential key to not getting lost—Watch Where You Are Going.

Perhaps this sounds like an oversimplification. Maybe. But that's what makes it so beautiful. There are no complicated theorems and nothing to memorize. Just stay in touch with the world you walk through. Be aware of details, and your chances of getting where you want to go, and back, are pretty good.

That range, too, ran into the northwest, becoming fainter and finally vanishing into the dim blue distance; it ran parallel with the granite range, and it had to be the Yukon-Northwest Territories divide. Divide to what? I wondered, peering through the glass—for neither of these ranges was marked on the map, and the map itself was a beautiful blank with the Flat River represented by a dotted line in the wrong place. That was the charm of that map: one might chance upon almost anything in those empty, uncrowded spaces.

—Dangerous River
R.M. Patterson
Chelsea Green Publishing Co., 1990

Sometimes the difficult part is knowing exactly *which* details to be aware of. But you can learn that, too—you'll find them all in the pages of this book.

So begin here. Before you jump ahead to the more-or-less mechanical techniques that look like quick-fix solutions, build the foundation of good judgment, that not-so-common sixth sense.

Locating Your Sixth Sense

I'd like to be able to encourage you with the good news that we all have, hidden deep within us, an innate ability to find our way; that during evolution we were left with some spare parts from the homing pigeon. But we haven't, and weren't. Or at least that is the way conservative, rigorous researchers in this field see things.

Others, however, remain unconvinced, and every once in a while come up with some rather promising (or at least entertaining) theories. My favorite is the revelation that we really can follow our noses. Scientists have discovered that we all have traces of iron in our noses located in the ethmoid bone (the one between the eyes). Some suggest that these trace deposits help us find direction relative to the earth's magnetic field.

A researcher at the University of Manchester, in England, found that when magnets were placed on the right side of a person's head the subject would tend to veer, by an obvious amount, to the right. Magnets on the left side drew the subjects to the left. This proved, or so the researchers claimed, that we are affected by magnetic fields. Many other animals, such as dolphins, tuna, sea turtles, salamanders, and bees have similar magnetic deposits near their brains, perhaps to help them navigate their way through life. There are also certain single-celled organisms that always swim toward the north side of a test dish.

The ability to sense direction became a minor scientific obsession in the mid-1800s. In 1873, a respected journal invited contributions on the topic, getting responses from such luminaries as Charles Darwin. The contributors agreed that man and animals probably made use of some instinctive direction-finding ability. None could cite any verifiable evidence, however. Instead, they used phrases like "guided by a kind of unerring instinct."

During the same period, medical science delved for the first time into the world of the blind, making it an active area of research. Of great fascination was the ability of blind people to avoid obstacles while finding their way. It was thought that the loss of one sense might enhance the others, or that it might bring forth the presence of a

completely new one. Many studies were performed, and one of them, done in 1905 by Emile Jarval, gave us the term "sixth sense." Jarval was convinced that this new sense was similar to our tactile sensations, except that rather than physical contact with an object it required the projection of "ether waves."

While this may sound strange to modern ears, Jarval's theory was tame compared with those of some of his contemporaries, who went completely otherworldly and mystical in their explanations. In all fairness, though, it is a baffling phenomenon. Lest we judge these experimenters too harshly, we should consider how many of us, when watching a blind person wend his or her way, find it hard not to believe that something inexplicable is occurring.

It is true that many blind people can perceive the presence of large objects and judge their distance from them with a surprising degree of accuracy. They do this by becoming more attuned to the differences in sound as it bounces back from their surroundings with a rudimentary form of echolocation. No instinctive powers are brought forth, no ether waves, just highly developed, highly trained natural senses.

To date, science has shown no evidence of a naturally occurring sixth sense of direction. Yet we still want to believe that it exists. We all know at least one person who never seems to get lost. It seems that there should be some explanation for this.

Probably the most pervasive, and persuasive, arguments are leftovers from the era of European exploration and colonization. Adventurers took home stories of so-called primitives who could navigate through dense forests or over featureless seas with no mechanical aids. The peculiar thing is that the tales about these great native trackers become more frequent as the European explorers became increasingly dependent on technology. Ancient writings in the East and West make no mention of any extraordinary ability to navigate. Perhaps it was taken for granted. But, as European civilization removed itself further and further from nature, the more astounding these feats appeared. It was a sign of awareness that an old world was disappearing, and with it, perhaps, old navigational skills.

By 1768, Captain James Cook, one of history's great navigators, had at his disposal the sextant for calculating latitude, a dependable chronometer to find longitude, astronomical tables, the best charts of the time, and a good working knowledge of how the earth was laid out. On a map of the world he could accurately place himself within a few miles, no matter where he was. The system he used (which in principle is the same used by modern navigators) was an abstract way of defining a position. It is based on locating yourself on an artificial grid made up of lines of latitude and longitude. The system works quite well, especially for those not familiar with the part of the world they find themselves in. It worked so well that Cook, and most others of his time, began to think it was the only way to navigate.

So it can be understood with what wonder the captain beheld his Polynesian guides. How, he thought, could these islanders find tiny atolls hundreds of miles across a trackless ocean with none of his fine gear and knowledge? The only explanation was that these children of nature still possessed a special sense civilized man had lost long ago. It was an attractive and romantic theme, and it got great play back home.

In truth, the guides he encountered had their own, equally valid system of navigation. Theirs was a more direct way of defining a position, accomplished through intimate experience rather than abstract thought.

In their system, you start from any known position and travel a certain distance in a set direction. If you know how far away something is and in what direction it lies, you know where it is in relation to you. In Cook's system a position was absolute; in their system a position was always relative. Accumulate enough of these directions and distances, and you define the world and your position in it. There were no secret or extra senses, just repeated travels and a great awareness of the world they lived in.

What seemed like a sixth sense to the Europeans was only an ability to discern direction and distance. For direction, Polynesian navigators used the heavens, winds, waves, plants, and a whole guidebook full of subtle, but learnable, signs. For calculating distance they had to look within themselves.

To many people of the world, distance is flexible. The Polynesians had no word for distance as such. They used time—the time it took to get somewhere. That was less abstract and easier to comprehend.

In practical terms, of course, it makes no difference how you measure it. Defining a distance as twenty miles can be just as useful as saying it's a two-day walk. But time is sometimes a handier way to express distance because we all have a natural sense of rhythm. We sense time with an internal rhythm or pulse, and it is the one "extra" sense that has been substantiated. Humans are just one of many species having a sense of the passage of time. A bee, for instance, not only knows its travel times, but can share this information with other bees. Many of us can tell the time with fair accuracy without looking at our watches, or estimate how long we have been at a job. It's a good, built-in measuring system, though it can be distorted by fatigue, heightened physical effort, or low blood sugar.

Cook and his Polynesian guides were equally good navigators. Each had a system that worked well. Yet the Europeans, out of conceit, refused to believe that others might have a knowledge equal

believing this to be an essential point in the geography of this western part of the Continent I determined to remain at all events untill I obtained the necessary data for fixing it's latitude. Longitude &c.

—The Journals of Lewis and Clark
Edited by Bernard De Voto
Houghton Mifflin Company, 1953

to their own. So they attributed it to primal instincts, something that came before knowledge. From this arrogance and misunderstanding sprang the myth of a sense of direction.

Now, after centuries of experience, we can learn from both systems of navigation. Later in the book we will navigate by Cook's abstract (absolute) positioning, and his guides' direct (relative) positioning. As you might imagine, there are advantages and disadvantages to both.

What has passed for a sense of direction is nothing more than careful observation and accumulated knowledge, things we are all capable of doing. Explorers were astounded by the memories of the Pacific islanders, Australian aborigines, and the Indians of North America for the smallest details of a landscape. While we might be capable of doing the same, modern life does not encourage it. Since these traits aren't needed to survive, they are not taught or passed on. Yet we can still tune in to this way of thinking and learn to see.

We can also learn to open up our other senses. With some concentration you can tap into, and become aware of, sounds and smells as well as what can be seen. While most of our information for direction finding is gathered by sight, studies show that smells and sounds can also be useful. Smells, in particular, imprint themselves in our memories. Some people claim that smell is the most sensitive sense, and the last to leave us in death. So open your ears and nose as well as your eyes when observing landmarks on the trail.

We all have the ability to remember these details and apply them to finding our way, although some people seem better able to do so than others. One person might remember routes previously traveled by relying on specific landmarks. In driving to a friend's house, he would turn left at the faded blue building, right at the park with broken swings, and left at the dry cleaners.

But someone else might use a different method, keeping track of how long she's traveled and in what direction. To get to that same friend's house, she might use her internal clock to drive in one direction for three minutes, turn left, go a short distance at forty miles an hour, turn right, and then drive for thirty seconds before making a final left turn.

Neither system is superior, and neither group gets lost more often than the other. There are different ways of navigating, and very often there is an overlapping of the two methods. The fact that the latter group does not rely on external signals just might be a reason why some people are loath to admit they are lost or to ask directions. To their senses, at least, they are right on track with no clues to tell them otherwise—they have no reason to feel lost.

The former group's affinity for distinct landmarks may be the reason some people have trouble reading maps. Since they respond better to complicated chains of landmarks, and not to distances and direction (the defining parameters of a map), they may be at a disadvantage when the only navigational help is a map. Or maybe it's just that some people are less likely to be exposed to mapreading when young. Certainly anyone can become an expert mapreader.

The hormones in your brain dictate the way you navigate and the techniques that work best for you. Those hormones affect the way we experi-

It is only the scholar who appreciates that all history consists of successive excursions from a single starting-point, to which man returns again and again to organize yet another search for a durable scale of values.

—A Sand County Almanac
Aldo Leopold
Oxford University Press, 1968

ence the world and the way we compile our mental maps (we'll have more to say about mental mapping later). So when you begin your studies on finding your way, think about how you remember where you are going. If you favor one method over another, use it.

Regardless of chemistry, we all acquire our wayfinding skills gradually. The great Polynesian navigators started their educations as small children. Even with all the information in this book, it will take time to develop your abilities and to sense what is out there. It can't be rushed. So enjoy the experience of getting disoriented every once in a while, and the pleasure of finding your way back.

A good way to start feeling your way around a new environment is to follow the example of most wandering tribespeople. They get their sense of direction in small doses, exploring the world around them a little at a time. This has often been referred to as a *home-based system*, using home as a constant point of reference. From their villages, they continually wander out and back. Each trip is a little longer and in alternating directions. As they travel, they gather details for their ever-expanding mental maps, piecing together a complex image of their world. Since they always maintain a mental link to their home base, they rarely get lost.

This type of wayfinding-by-exploration is reassuring in that there is always a connection to where you started. Security comes from its thread of continuity, which is why it is also known as the Principle of Ariadne's Thread. In Greek mythology, Ariadne gave her lover, Theseus, a ball of thread to unwind as he entered the Minotaur's labyrinth. After killing the beast, he escaped by following the thread. Hansel and Gretel's trail of breadcrumbs was a similar method, one also reputedly used by the Indians of British Columbia who, when conditions were right, dropped cedar chips in the wakes of their canoes to mark the way home in thick fog.

The problem with the home-based system is that you can't just show up at an unfamiliar location and begin to find your way around. But it can be adapted to serve this purpose. Instead of

He reached the summit of the plateau beyond Comb Wash, left the old road and headed south, guiding himself by the stars. The going was rough, rocky, over a highly irregular surface cut up by draws, gullies and ravines, some of them tending west, others east back to Comb Wash. Hayduke tried to follow the divide between the two drainage systems—not easy in the dark, in a piece of back country where he had never set foot before.

—The Monkey Wrench Gang
Edward Abbey
Avon Books, 1976

home, you relate all directions to any prominent local feature, or *landmark*. This feature can be a central point, such as a building or mountain, or a long line, like a river or road. Using your chosen reference point or line to make a mental map brings you very close to thinking and finding your way like those "primitives" with their magical sense of direction.

These techniques emphasize an important point: You need to use something other than yourself as a reference. A good way to get lost is to relate to the world in terms of yourself: "That mountain is to my left, the river is behind me." As you move through the world, the position of these objects changes in relation to you. It's easy to get confused, and then lost. A better way is to think on a grander scale. Look for a constant reference that never moves and keep relating back to it. We've already done this with a home base or a local feature, and we'll discover many others in the following chapters.

This ability to experience your environment

from a *geocentric perspective* (your position relative to the world) rather than an *egocentric perspective* (the world's position relative to you) is a step in the right direction. Done on a regular basis, it can even keep you from getting disoriented. For example, in one case study a young man never seemed to make any deliberate efforts to orient himself and yet rarely got lost in a strange city. The explanation came from his early training. For some reason, his mother had always given him directions using the points of the compass, rather than the more usual left or right. She would say "Get me the brush on the north (instead of right) side of the dresser," or "sit in the chair on the east side of the porch." Eventually the young man developed an unusual ability to move in a complicated path for relatively long periods and retain his orientation without paying attention to it. He saw himself as moving within the world. He didn't perceive the world to be moving around him. In this way he always remained properly oriented.

Long ago, the state of being oriented meant to face the east, toward the rising sun (hence the origin of the word *Orient*). You aligned yourself with everything else through that one constant direction. We now use north (and south) for orienting because it is more convenient to find north from the stars or with a compass. Like the young man in the above example, as long as you can stay aligned with some external reference it will be easier to keep track of where you are.

Although we have no innate sense of direction, we can develop the ability to stay oriented. Practice is essential. Use what you feel comfortable with and what comes naturally. Try to combine observed landmarks, memorable details, direction and distance covered, and points or lines of reference. Practice every day, no matter where you are.

How Not to Get Lost

You'll find that it won't take long before you, too, can locate what will convincingly pass for a genuine sense of direction.

In the previous section we discovered that while we are not born with a sense of direction, it can be acquired. By learning to stay aware of our surroundings and by maintaining a reference to some constant, we should be able to avoid getting lost. I also alluded to the fact that there are some simple ways to do this. Here they are.

Bear in mind that there is no one correct or "right" technique for finding your way. The proper method is to use all methods. Employ what is at hand, what you feel sure about. During an outing, opportunities will arise to use a variety of skills. The more you know, the better off you'll be, and the less anxious you will be about getting lost. Learn when you can. Practice what you learn. And use it all.

Here's an example of what I mean. Two friends making a cross-country flight in a small plane had very different personalities and ways of keeping track of where they were. One loved gadgets. She had all sorts of electronic gear that told her where she was and where she was going. She never had to look out the window. Her partner had the opposite approach. He looked for landmarks, kept track of time and distance, observed the sun and wind, and ignored the instruments. At a given time, both agreed to point to where they thought they were on the map. When the time came they were both right.

They were also both wrong. A better way to avoid getting lost would have been to use *everything* they had. Watch the electronics, look at the landscape, monitor the compass, and read the map. This way, if one system fails or seems questionable, you have backups. This also allows you to evaluate your judgment objectively by comparing information from various sources. In navigation, you can never have too much information.

The technical methods of finding your way with map and compass will be explained later in this book. All you will need for those chapters is some inexpensive gear and some practice using it. For now, though, let's build up your basic wayfinding skills so you can make the kind of educated judgments that form the foundation of a dependable sense of direction.

The need for these basic skills begins even before you take your first step in the wilderness. When you find yourself entering a situation in which you might get lost—such as starting a hike (or arriving in a new city, or walking into a shopping mall)—go no farther until you have picked out an easily identifiable feature that can be used as a reference. This can be a single point, like a mountain; or a line, like a coast, river, or road. It can be something that is always visible to you as you travel, or something whose existence is known only from a map. Without delay, locate yourself in terms of direction and distance to this reference. Now you know where your starting point is, and your journey can begin.

Your job is to keep track of your reference and where you are in relation to it.

If the reference is a point, your routes will radiate from it, spiral around it, or vector past it. If it is a line, think of it as a tree with branches leading out from and back to a central trunk, or with vines hanging parallel to the trunk.

A line is the handier of the two references because it lets you set up crossing lines (the tree's branches), giving you four primary directions. When using a compass the main reference line is the north/south axis, from which you also get a perpendicular east/west line. You can do the same with any other reference line such as a river, a range of hills, a coastline, a logging road, or a valley.

In a city you might use a street as your main reference line. New York has Fifth Avenue, a main artery that runs the length of the city. This then becomes your uptown/downtown reference line, from which you also get crosstown lines perpendicular to it.

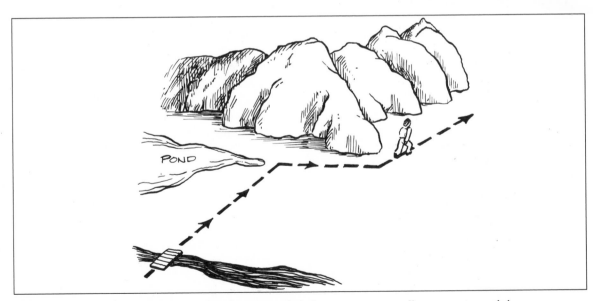

Repeating patterns. *This hiker knows that the streams along her route run generally west to east, and the hills trend south and north, so she is heading generally north. Every so often she compares her map with the surrounding view, locating landmarks and checking her position. She glances at her compass when necessary. Though her approach seems casual, through attention to the landscape she knows where she is at all times.*

Repeating patterns offer another type of reference line. These can be used in place of one central line, or for keeping yourself on course when not in sight of your main reference. A pattern could be any series of features. This could be a series of rivers running parallel—or roughly so—to your main reference line. Or it could be streams (or streets) running into your reference line. For instance, most mountain ranges in the U.S. run north and south. The streams running from them usually trend east and west. Smaller patterns can be found in the way snow or sand drifts with the prevailing wind. Patterns are everywhere. Use them.

Animals use naturally occurring reference lines, and so can you. Wildebeests follow ridges and rivers. Caribou travel along valleys or tree lines. Lemmings cross ice-covered lakes by keeping mountains to one side. And pigeons use the sun's shadow (a line) for orientation. You should try the same.

When traveling toward a goal, as from a cabin to a lake, decide on a route and try to stick to it; if midcourse corrections are necessary, make them deliberate, definite, and retraceable. This way, even if you can't find the lake, you'll at least be able to retrace your steps to the cabin. If you just go out there and wander aimlessly, you might miss the lake *and* the cabin.

A lake is a good target to aim for because it's big. In contrast, a campsite by the lake would be a poor target, for it is relatively small and therefore harder to find. If you aimed for the campsite, how would you know in which direction to turn if you missed it? You wouldn't.

But if you aimed for the lake, or a part of it (such as "the end nearest the hills") you'd no doubt hit it. Then all you'd have to do would be to follow the shoreline toward the camp. To avoid getting lost, aim at a big target. Don't go for a hole in one. Just get to the green and putt your way home from there.

When you intend to wander about rather than strike off toward a specific goal, you won't be able to stick to a set route. For this sort of traveling, an easily recognizable reference is even more important, because it's all you'll have. You can use either a point or a line. With a point, head out and back over ever-increasing distances, gathering information and improving your knowledge of the area on each excursion. Or, if the point is always visible, like a tall mountain or building, you can wander as you will. As long as it stays in sight, you're OK. When you're working with a line, stay to one side of it while walking generally in a direction that is parallel to it. For example, wander about on one side of a river (or road), always heading upstream (or uptown). When you've had enough, return to the line and follow it downstream (or downtown) to where you started.

While underway, think of what you and the world around you would look like to a bird overhead. Envision the larger picture and your place in it. This is your mental map. Do this by continually updating your position through the use of sequential landmarks, or by keeping track of how far and in what directions you have gone.

Experiment with your internal rhythm, your natural ability to judge time (which is as useful in navigation as is distance traveled). Experiments show that many animals can measure time to an accuracy of .3 percent. In other words, they would be no more than three minutes out after a period of sixteen hours and forty minutes.

Humans do not have such extraordinary accuracy. But, with practice, we can come to within ten minutes (although not consistently) in twelve hours—which is good enough in a pinch. Sharpen your skills at estimating time by trying to guess what time it is, or how long you have been doing something. By all means take your watch with you on the trail, but tune in your innate sense of time as you tune in your other senses.

Above all, stay aware of the world you are moving through. Every once in a while, turn off the radio in the car, or stop talking on the trail. Watch where you are going and don't just follow the boots ahead of you. Look around constantly.

A good trick is to try to remember important features by their shape rather than color. Our brains retain forms better than hues and tones.

But don't just depend on what you see. Use all five senses—combining them into a sixth.

Use your ears. Chain saws, church bells, cars on a highway, trains, the clang of industry, farm animals, the roar of rapids, or the crash of surf are all capable in the right circumstances of giving clues to your position. To judge more accurately from which direction a sound is coming, use only one ear, or cup your hands around both, while slowly turning. You'll be able to come within ten degrees, which is pretty good.

Use your nose. Sailors often speak of smelling land before they see it. Water smells, too. The moisture from any body of water, be it river or ocean, produces a distinctive aroma. Odors from new-mowed lawns, farms, freshly turned earth, wildflowers, factories, oil refineries, and car exhausts can drift long distances downwind. They're often strongest in fog, mist, or rain.

Don't try to take in or remember every little peculiarity. Your memory can't store or use that much information. Don't bother with anything other than the most obvious features beyond your immediate route. Save your concentration for the finer details along your present path. As you proceed, turn around at every junction and landmark. Study what you see. This will be the view you'll encounter on your return trip. Think in reverse to maintain the Ariadne Thread that will take you back.

It's always safest to stay on marked roads or trails, and not leave them unless you are positive you know where you are and how to reach your destination. Trails may seem boring but they offer the best chance of taking you where you want to go and back. (In many wilderness areas, we are requested to stay on marked trails for another reason, too: to minimize disturbance to surrounding areas, which may include nesting sites, thin soil vulnerable to erosion, or scarce habitat.)

Stay with a trail until it either disappears or heads persistently in the wrong direction. Then head back, or start some serious navigating. Beware of old or marginal-looking trails, which have a way of petering out at inconvenient times. Game trails often lead to nothing more than good forage. Even on a trail it is good wayfinding procedure to stay in touch with where you are, to take note of landmarks you pass, to relate your position to references, and to remember distances and directions traveled. Trail intersections that look well marked and obvious may look different when approached from the opposite direction. Maintain a running record in your mind of the path you have followed. If the route has been indirect, you might even keep written notes or make simple sketch maps (we'll see how later on). This gives both your present position and the way to get back.

All of this envisioning process, and a mosaic of observations, is stored in your gray matter as what we have been calling a "mental map." This map is nothing more than an outline of shapes, directions of paths and roads, prominent landmarks, and relative positions of everything in it. Everyone has a substantial catalog of them, one for each place we've been and many for places we only dream about. Some are too old to read, others are fresh and accurate, and all are unlike anyone else's— because we each see the world differently.

When I had gone quite a distance over the rocks—far enough, I thought, to be down on the plateau—I stopped and looked around. I couldn't see anything that looked like a trail. I couldn't find a single spot of white paint. I thought I must be down on the plateau, but could not be sure. . . . Boy, it's no fun getting off the trail, when the cloud is so thick you can't see a dozen yards ahead!

—Lost on a Mountain in Maine
Donn Fendler
The Welles Publishing Company, Inc., 1939

It's important to cultivate the ability to create mental maps. But I'll guarantee that what's in your head isn't exactly a Rand McNally atlas. Since we each see the world from a unique perspective, our mental maps are not as accurate as we might like to think—we'll find out why in the next section. Still, practice "drawing" and reading them. They're a great help.

The common link between the loose bits of information in this section is staying aware of your surroundings and maintaining a reference to a constant. With these two principles in mind, you shouldn't get lost. But don't just take this information and store it away. Use it in your daily life as you drive to work, pass through a city, enter a new airport terminal, or walk in the park. Practice is important, for navigation in the wilderness or anywhere else is not a technique—it's a habit, a manner of thinking, and an awareness of the land. It's seeing indicators, and noticing what is going on around you.

Why We Get Lost

Under the definition of "lost" we come across such dismal synonyms as helpless, desperate, denied, and even insensible. You may be one of the few people on the planet who has never felt this aimless despair, but for the rest of us these words hit home. The question then is: If getting lost is so awful, why do we let it happen to us? In part, the answer is that we can't help ourselves.

We seem to have an almost natural ability to do it, which probably makes getting lost our real sixth sense. For a start, we can't even walk in a straight line. Try it. Go to a beach, a field of snow, or any open area where you will leave footprints. Make sure there is no wind or bright sun to act as a reference point. Now blindfold yourself and try to walk a straight line. You'll probably find that after an eighth of a mile your track has begun to veer. At half a mile there is a noticeable curve, and after a few miles you might cross your own tracks—making a complete circle. And if you walked faster, the circle would tighten.

Actually it would be remarkable if we didn't walk in circles. It's in our bones—literally. Each of us is built slightly lopsided and asymmetrical. Without visual clues to guide us in a straight line, these imbalances take over and we head off in circles. The most common cause, having the greatest effect, is that one leg is shorter than the other. There seems to be no dominant side. You are as likely to deviate to the left as to the right. And, for no apparent reason, men tend to stray about half as much as women.

Of course there are those who can't, or won't, accept the obvious. One scientist theorized that there was a natural spiraling influence in the brain of all living creatures. Maybe, but it is the more mundane reasons, such as legs of slightly different length, that actually throw us off course.

Another factor, though less detrimental, is that we usually favor one eye. Instead of looking at a distant object equally through both eyes, we depend on one more than the other. This makes it harder to walk a straight path.

We also angle away from things that bother us. We take the course of least resistance without being aware of it. Wind, rain, and snow from one side will make us tend toward the other. We also naturally veer downhill, never uphill. When we come across a minor obstruction we usually step around it toward our favored side. And, when given a choice, ninety-eight percent of us turn right. Do this enough times and you have begun to go seriously off course.

We rarely have to travel in an absolutely straight line, of course, so this inability is not critical. Admittedly, you might try to cross an open expanse toward a distant landmark, lose it in the haze, and become disoriented. But that is exceptional and there are ways of making sure it doesn't happen, as you'll learn later.

Don't be tempted to wander off into the unknown depending on a vague assurance that "this feels like the right way." Depend on reliable facts. And beware of unreliable facts. Where do unreliable facts come from? Unfortunately, one of the main sources is your head.

In the previous section we spoke of mental maps, data banks of stored information about how different parts of our world are pieced together. Everyone has them. Some are better than others. The problem with these maps is that they are based not only on your direct experiences, but on your indirect ones as well. This means that a lot of what is stored up there has been passed on from secondhand sources.

Books, television, photos, real maps, and conversations (descriptions of other people's mental maps) all help to sketch out the maps in your mind. It's inevitable. You can't be everywhere, so you must sometimes depend on outside sources. This is not necessarily bad. But problems arise when our maps are influenced by our prejudices, imagination, and unique perceptions.

For instance, you might read a guidebook that comments on landmarks on a trail, or on sights along the way. From the written words, you'll build an image of what you expect to see. But it's not always what you'll find. If you force yourself to be objective, though, you'll probably have to agree that what was written was an accurate description, and that it was you who read something else into it. This is perfectly normal. We concoct images not so much from the way things are, but the way we think they are, or should be. The two are often very different. Be prepared to revise your preconceptions when they no longer fit your surroundings.

Even when we look at something directly, we constantly modify the information and redraw our mental maps to fit our interpretations. Psychologists say that much of what we imagine to be true about our surroundings is actually unsupported or inferred information. Our mental maps are therefore part fact and part fiction. They comprise haphazardly gathered material from direct and indirect sources, often altered to fit our preconceived notions.

To see what I mean, try this: Draw a map of a familiar area and then compare it to a professionally drawn map. You'll begin to get an idea of how biased your vision of the world is. You'll draw what you know best with great accuracy, leave out what is unimportant to you, and often alter size and distance to express your priorities.

This doesn't mean you should ignore the maps in your mind. Far from it. They're a vital part of developing a sense of direction, and you need them for a bird's-eye view of where you are. Just don't let them run riot. Keep them under control from the start. Learn to edit them. Fine-tune your mental maps with information from real (cartographic) maps, a compass, landmarks, and reference points and lines. One of the easiest ways of getting lost is to put too much trust in your unedited mental map and to let your "feelings" overcome your informed good judgment.

The manner in which we "read" cartographic maps is also colored by desire or preconception. We may well envision a landscape that doesn't exist, or convince ourselves that a tempting trail isn't going to be too steep to follow. It is the same with photos of an area we want to explore, or a description of a goal or landmark. All can be transformed by our preconceived notions of what we believe things should look like. We've all seen the standard photo of the Matterhorn. That is our image of it. But if we came upon it from a different angle, would the image and the reality mesh?

Information is even more likely to become confused when transferred by the spoken word, as when getting directions. Very often we hear something very different from what was said. It happens all the time. Of course it is just as likely that those giving the directions don't know what they're talking about in the first place.

Be particularly cautious when asking locals for directions. People who live where you are traveling are often not interested in the same things you are. While they can tell you how to get to a market or a drinking well, they may not know where a scenic waterfall is. They may have heard of it or visited it once long ago, but it is not part of their

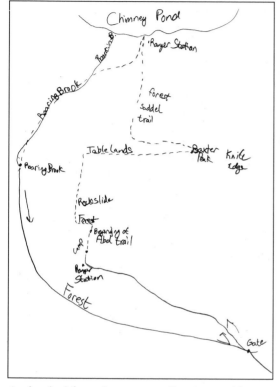

As sketched from the memory of a 12-year-old.

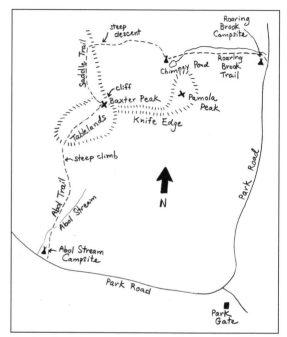

As sketched from the memory of a 42-year-old.

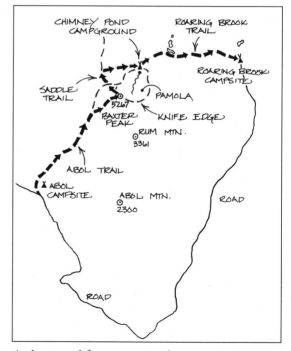

And as traced from a topographic map.

The trail from Abol Stream campground (Baxter State Park, Maine) to Baxter Peak on Mt. Katahdin, then to Chimney Pond campground, then to Roaring Brook campground.

Because our mental maps are imperfect, we must be willing to adjust them when necessary. Note that the older hiker (who was reading a map during the hike) has his directions approximately correct, but his distances are suspect.

daily experience. This is true of all peoples, primitive or civilized. Most Parisians couldn't offer you more than the vaguest instructions on how to get to the Louvre, but could give precise directions to a local bank or wine shop.

Then there is pride, which often prevents people from admitting they don't know the way. When you ask for directions, they improvise; sometimes they'll tell you it's impossible to get there from here.

Asking for directions and picking up local knowledge is half the fun of getting lost. You get colorful advice and meet lots of new folks (whom you will never be able to find again, of course). Don't be too anxious to believe what others tell you. Integrate local knowledge with what you know for sure from your map or compass. And be wary of asking strangers to pinpoint a place on your map. Many are not familiar with maps. They'll jab a finger down anywhere, just to save face and get rid of you.

It's human nature not to admit that you don't know where something is. It's just as difficult to admit you're lost. The cover-up urge is stronger in some of us than others. Yet it is important to recognize this shortcoming and acknowledge it when you feel the slight twinge of being disoriented. Don't wait for the twinge to develop into the full-blown panic of being lost. Ignoring the reality that you *may* be lost is a good way to get thoroughly lost.

We often have no control over the causes of our getting lost, the causes we've just been discussing. They are (to varying degrees) a part of us. So there is an excuse for it. But there is no excuse for getting lost when it can be prevented—that is, when it is only our failure to use good navigational techniques that gets us into trouble.

This usually happens when we forget to keep track of our position. You say to yourself, "I'm only going a short distance. Why bother?" It can occur when you're taking a shortcut off the trail, or going for a brief stroll away from camp. Then there are those who see no reason to bother with all that navigating stuff because they are always going to stick to the trails. The fault with that rea-

soning is that trails have a way of disappearing, or of being hard to find in the first place. Things are rarely as easy as they look.

Many trails start at the junction of back roads, which themselves are hard to follow and often lead into complex mazes. Then, too, trails cross each other, markers or blazes may be missing or destroyed, or deer or other large animals may have made their own paths that look inviting.

The clearly marked trail on your park map, which looks so obvious and easy to follow, may in reality be old, overgrown, or not much of a trail to start with. Even on a well-marked trail you can get lost by not watching where you are going. If the going on a trail is rough we tend to watch the ground directly ahead of us. This makes it easy to miss a turn or go off on an unmarked path. Or you may encounter a well-blazed or well-cairned trail made by someone when they were lost. It happens. In fact, it's common. Then too, if you don't keep track of where you are, you can lose your feeling for direction when visibility is suddenly limited. Fog, rain, night, or snow can make a trail disappear very quickly. Then what?

Off the trail, beaten path, or streets of a familiar city, we lose our way by not clinging to the basic tenets of staying found. You must immediately establish, then maintain, a reference, keep track of directions and distances traveled, remember landmarks, or aim for a broad target. If you don't, you're a prime candidate for not getting home for supper.

We get lost not because of what we do, but because of what we don't do. You stay oriented primarily by keeping track of where you are. This is not complicated to do, only taking a bit of time and effort. Every fifteen minutes, or whenever you change direction, estimate where you are. If you're the methodical type, keep track of your position with notes ("turned west at crossed dead trees, walked twelve minutes to abandoned tractor"). And if you plan to return along the same route, turn around frequently to see what your path will look like on the way back. Watch where you are going.

How to "Get Found"

Well, now you've done it. You've been daydreaming, seeing the sights. Now you've turned a corner and realized you haven't a clue where you are. Fifteen minutes ago you felt yourself hesitate at a junction; ten minutes later you didn't recognize an obvious landmark. You were merely disoriented then. But now you're lost. You can't figure out how to retrace your steps; everything looks the same. Nothing seems familiar. OK, now what are you going to do?

The first thing is to stop. Don't keep on walking and making things worse. Admit that you are lost and that it's probably only going to be a small inconvenience, not a life-threatening episode. Calm yourself. Sit down, have a bite to eat, clear your head, and begin looking for clues. Try to remember where you have been during the last half-hour. Envision the last point where you were sure of your position.

Look around for features that might provide a reference. If nothing registers, but you think that you are not far from somewhere familiar, start navigating from scratch. Identify a landmark, or make one, for your current position so you can find it again. Head out from there to explore a little at a time, returning if unsuccessful. For more detailed information, look ahead to "When You Are Lost" in Chapter 5.

Since the beginning of long-distance flying, aviators have filed flight plans at their points of departure. These forms list the names of those traveling, their destination, their intended route, gear carried, time of departure, and estimated time of arrival. When they don't show up, the folks back home at least have an idea what cornfield the wreckage might be in. The system has helped rescuers find many a downed aircraft, and there is no reason not to use the same approach when hiking in a national park or the great unknown. And if you do file a travel plan, make sure to tell the folks that you're back. (Caution: Don't leave a travel plan under the windshield wiper of your car at the trailhead. It's an invitation to thieves. There might be no car to come back to.)

The thought that he was lost fell upon Bullock with the suddenness of a marauder. One moment he was jogging along with eyes on the swaying sled, the next he was scanning the horizon in search of something familiar. His back was torturing him, but he dared not stop. The fact that his dogs might lead him to safety found no place in his consciousness.

—Snow Man
Malcolm Waldron
Houghton Mifflin Company, 1931

When it's obvious that you are lost, try what you can to reorient yourself. If it's hopeless, don't try heading off on a hunch. This is the worst time to start trusting your sixth sense. It's probably what got you lost in the first place. Either use proven navigational techniques to find something you recognize, or start making it easy for others to find you.

And next time, do yourself a favor. Watch where you are going, and where you have been.

Chapter Two

MAPS

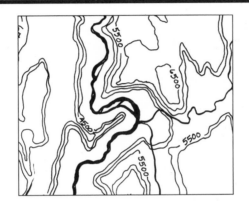

Maps

After learning to understand road signs, the first navigational tool we are introduced to is the map. We all grow up with them, which is what makes it so strange that there are so many "cartophobes" among us. In this chapter we'll learn what maps can do and, maybe more important, what they can't. We'll see what truths they hold and how they lie. First, though, you'll need to learn the language and vocabulary of map symbols. Like books, maps are meant to be read, but a map gives you all its information at once instead of doling it out a page at a time. The trick is to learn how to absorb it in small doses.

Another disorienting attribute of maps is that they convert the full-sized three-dimensional world into a greatly reduced flat one you can hold in your hand. It is up to the map reader to re-expand and inflate that tiny, flat landscape in his mind's eye, and the conceptual gymnastics required for this take practice—more so because maps are drawn as if for birds looking down at the world, rather than for earth-bound creatures like us.

So we'll find out how to identify from the side all the features maps depict from above. And finally, we'll explore the arcane art of map folding.

A word of warning, however: This chapter will be wasted if you don't get out there with map in hand, wander around, get lost, get found, and see what maps are all about. Read and practice; by the end of this chapter you'll be a master.

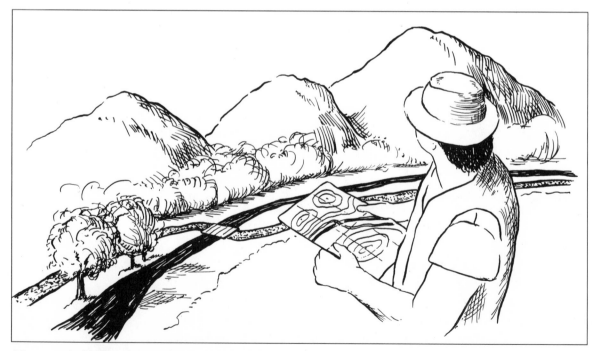

Map properly folded and oriented with the landscape.

The World in Your Hands

Once you understand their language, maps speak volumes. They show what can't be seen, identify what you can see, help plan your route, pick a campsite, warn of potential hazards, lead you to areas of beauty, and, by providing directions and distances to known landmarks, pinpoint your position.

The modern cartographer's art creates an accurate and comprehensive document that, with practice, is easier to read than the explanations that follow. Good maps are the quintessential explainers, part of our way of thinking. We "map out" plans of attack. We ask plaintively if we have to "draw a map" when describing something.

Many of us have never learned to read maps because there seemed to be no need. We blindly follow the road signs or the blazes on a trail. But if we miss a sign or stray from the path, we're in trouble. Wayfinding then becomes like playing an instrument without being able to read music. You can do it, but you'll always be handicapped.

Unfortunately, no map can be taken at pure face value. Maps have been called "truth compressed into symbols," and they need to be interpreted. They're not exact replicas, and therefore require imagination to get out what has been put in.

The navigator's job, as interpreter, is to compare the map with the real world. This is more than a simple exercise in spatial relationships. Envisioning the full-size, three-dimensional world greatly reduced and flat takes special ability, which comes only from practice.

Though maps offer a lot, no map can tell you everything. The best navigators are those who augment map data with as much outside information and experience as possible. They also plan ahead for alternative routes and landmarks in case what a map shows doesn't seem to be there.

Don't take any map literally, particularly with regard to road and trail systems, which tend to change between map editions. Look for significant features within the general pattern of details. To get the most out of maps, you must know when to go beyond them.

The Lie of the Land

Do maps lie? Not really—but sometimes they don't tell the whole truth. Remember Huck Finn and Tom Sawyer's balloon flight? Huck knew they were still over Illinois because the land below was green, not pink—which any fool knew was the color of Indiana.

When Tom asked what color had to do with it, Huck replied, "It's got everything to do with it. Illinois is green and Indiana is pink . . . I've seen it on the map, and it's pink."

When Tom questioned this interpretation, Huck said, " . . . well what's a map for? Ain't it to learn you facts?"

"Of course."

"Well then, how's it going to do that if it lies?"

In his own way, Huck was right. While some maps come close, none is perfectly accurate. They can't show every barn, chicken coop, or rock outcrop. Nor can they precisely indicate what a swamp, meadow, or woods will be like, or how the land changes. Impassable cliffs, for example, may lurk unmarked between contour lines.

New roads are always being built, and old trails overgrown. Maps more than a few years old may be substantially out of date. Change is constant.

Why, on some newfangled maps, Indiana ain't even pink no more.

Types of Maps

Maps are scaled-down representations of the earth's surface, and different types of maps do this in different ways.

The style with which you are probably most familiar is the planimetric map, which gets its name from the Latin words *planus* (even or flat) and *metrum* (measure). It represents the world as if it were all a level surface—without mountains or valleys, mesas or canyons—so there's a lot that planimetric maps aren't telling you. What they lose in natural features they make up for with information about man-made features.

For outdoor wayfinding, the least useful planimetric map is the grade school version, showing only towns and political boundaries—the kind Huck Finn was navigating by. A planimetric road map for autos is slightly more useful, and more useful still are the visitors' guides provided at parkgrounds and those available from the U.S. Forest Service and the National Park Services (see Appendix). These show trails, roads, streams, rivers, rangers' stations, and campgrounds in great detail. They are more than sufficient for finding your way in well-marked parks when you're sure you won't be leaving the trails.

The most useful maps for our purposes are *topographic* (top-oh-GRAPHic) maps. These describe the terrain—the shape of the landscape, its ups and downs—as well as some man-made features. They are ideal for hikers, campers, hunters, fishermen, cross-country skiers, and anyone else who may forsake the beaten path. They are of value even if you stick to the trails; by painting a more accurate perception of the landscape, they offer you a better chance to keep track of your position. Planimetrics will often show trails and roads that are not on topographics, and topographics will show natural features you won't find on a planimetric. If you can, carry both types, or transfer information to your topographic map before leaving.

There are topos (TOE-poes), as they are casually referred to, covering almost every square inch of the United States, its territories and protectorates, Canada, and a good part of the remaining world. In the U.S. they are compiled by the U.S.

Geological Survey (USGS), which now has a library of about 54,000 of them. You can purchase topos directly from the USGS by mail or phone, or from local outdoor shops (see the Appendix for map sources).

To make ordering easy, each state has been subdivided into *quadrangles*—commonly known as *quads*—based on lines of longitude and latitude. Simply choose the quad you want from a free state index. Quads are named for towns or prominent geographical features. USGS maps are made to extremely high standards: At least ninety percent of all points surveyed must be accurate to within one-fiftieth of an inch on the map. You won't miss much with a USGS topo for your guide. Costing only a few dollars, the maps are true bargains.

If you're traveling by water, maps are properly called charts. Nautical charts carry very little information about the land (usually only along the shore) but a lot about the water and what is under it. They show depths, bottom features, what the bottom is made of, and the positions of navigational aids such as buoys and lighthouses. The National Ocean Service compiles charts for coastal waters and the Great Lakes. The Army Corps of Engineers covers the navigable inland waterways, lakes, and rivers. For camping by canoe or kayak you can get by with just a topo, but when heading into open or coastal waters carry a nautical chart too.

There are other, more esoteric varieties of maps available—even enhanced aerial photos. But nothing beats the USGS topos for value, accuracy, and availability. We'll use them as a standard navigational tool throughout this book.

Since it takes almost five years to generate a new USGS topo, they are revised only when absolutely necessary. The last field check on the average topo may have been done about 30 years ago. Forest Service and Park Service maps, as well as some that are privately produced (such as the Trails Illustrated series), tend to be updated more frequently. Although even the latest map can be dated, it's the man-made features—including bridges, roads, trails, or campgrounds—that are

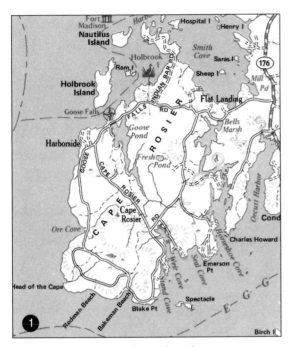

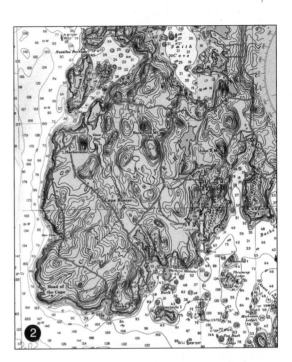

Cape Rosier, Maine, as depicted on three map types. Clockwise from top left: (1) a planimetric road map from Delorme Mapping Company's Maine Gazeteer; (2) a National Ocean Survey chart; and (3) a USGS topographic map. Each emphasizes different features.

most likely to change. Natural topographical features will rarely vary. It is wise to supplement maps with information from the latest guidebooks, park rangers, naturalists, and travelers you trust.

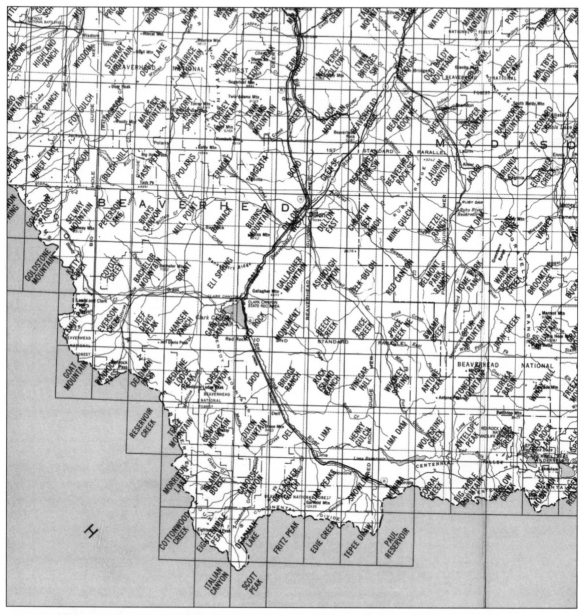

Choosing a map: Call or write the USGS (see Appendix) to get a free Index of Topographical Maps for the state you are traveling in. From another map, such as a road map, find the area of interest, noting names of towns or prominent natural features. Locate this area on the index by estimating its position and matching names. Shown here is part of the 7.5-minute topographical map coverage of Montana, taken from the USGS Montana Index. The index also shows the 1:50,000, 1:100,000, and 1:250,000 scale coverage of the state, and lists various specialty maps such as standard and shaded-relief 1:125,000 topos of Yellowstone National Park.

Three Dimensions Into Two

Maps take a god's-eye view of the world, looking down and seeing what we cannot. We mortals have limited horizons, seeing only small portions of the world from a decidedly lower point of view.

Relating the compressed, two-dimensional descriptions on a map to the three-dimensional full-sized world can be a daunting task for the imagination. At first, what is represented on the map will look nothing at all like the world around you. That is, until you learn to see.

Start by picking out obvious landmarks and finding your position among them. Next, judge the distances between landmarks, and then between them and yourself, to get a sense of scale. Do the same each time you use a map for a new area. It takes time to get the proper perspective, but it must be done or you'll confuse rivers with streams and hills with mountains.

A rugged Southwestern landscape as depicted on a topo map (simplified for reproduction purposes), below, and from a buzzard's-eye view, upper right. Your view south from the spot marked "X" would look like the lower right illustration.

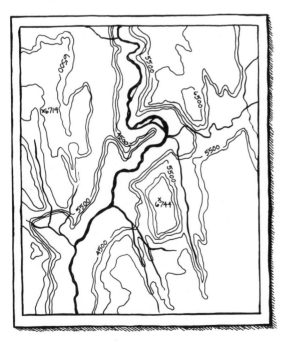

The Language of Maps

Part 1: Symbols

If we are successfully to interpret a map's message, we must first understand its language. And the language of maps is symbols. It's a purely visual and very descriptive means of communication that is done with a surprisingly modest vocabulary of lines, colors, and forms.

Shown here are the principal symbols, the basic vocabulary of the USGS "dictionary." The best way to make sense of them is to relate each symbol to what it represents.

Before going any further, get a map from any of the sources listed in the Appendix. You won't be able to understand the rest of this chapter unless you have a map in hand. Try to get a map of a nearby area, so you can walk about and compare the map with what is around you. First you learn to read, then to interpret.

Since cartographers try to make symbols look like what they represent, most are self-explanatory. This is why the symbols used in USGS topos are so similar to those found on maps from private companies as well as those from other nations. Canadian topos are very handy in that a complete list of symbol descriptions is printed on each map. U.S. maps have only a few listed. You are expected to carry the free pamphlet *Topographical Map Symbols* (see Appendix). For U.S. nautical charts, a complete book of symbols can be found in the NOS publication *Chart No. 1* (see Appendix).

To be legible, symbols are often drawn slightly oversized. The symbol for a school, for example, might be larger than the scale structure. Regardless of this, the middle of the symbol will always be over the location of the building's center.

Because of the width of printed lines, roads, trails, streams, and small rivers also may not be to scale. But their centerlines will be accurately plotted.

Color is used to enhance information or make it more obvious. The USGS has standardized its use of color as follows:

Black: Man-made features such as roads, trails, railroads, or buildings. Names are always in black.
Blue: Waterways such as lakes, rivers, canals, swamps, and marshes. The contour lines of glaciers and permanent snowfields are also blue.
Brown: Contour lines and elevations.
Green: Substantial vegetation, woods, scrub, orchards, or groves.
White: No vegetation, cleared land, or areas with sparse or scattered foliage.
Red: Larger, more important roads and surveying lines.
Purple: Overprinting. Revisions added from aerial photos but not yet field-checked.

Some state-produced maps make do with just one color. The USGS offers no monochromatic maps, while Canada has quite a few in both color and monochrome. These maps represent different areas in tones of gray. They are harder to interpret, but are cheaper and make better photocopies (handy for making copies for everyone on a trip). Notes in colored (red or blue) ink also stand out better.

Map reading is not an instinctive skill, it's an acquired one. It comes from the practice of comparing the world on the map with the one you see around you. To learn a language you must use it. Pick up a map, go outside, and look around. It will be an enjoyable education.

CONTROL DATA AND MONUMENTS

Boundary monument:

   With tablet . . . .   BM □ 71

BOUNDARIES

State or territorial . . . .

County or equivalent . . . .

Civil township or equivalent . . . .

Park, reservation, or monument . . . .

ROADS AND RELATED FEATURES

Primary highway . . . .

Secondary highway . . . .

Light duty road . . . .

Unimproved road . . . .

Trail . . . .

Bridge . . . .

Drawbridge . . . .

BUILDINGS AND RELATED FEATURES

Dwelling or place of employment: small; large . . .

School; church . . . .

Airport . . . .

Well (other than water); windmill . . . .

Water tank: small; large . . . .

Landmark object . . . .

Campground; picnic area . . . .

Cemetery: small; large . . . .   Cem

RAILROADS AND RELATED FEATURES

Standard gauge single track; station . . . .

CONTOURS

Topographic:

   Intermediate . . . .

   Index . . . .

   Depression . . . .

MINES AND CAVES

Quarry or open pit mine . . . .

Gravel, sand, clay, or borrow pit . . . .

Mine tunnel or cave entrance . . . .

SURFACE FEATURES

Sand or mud area, dunes, or shifting sand . . . . . .

Intricate surface area . . . .

Gravel beach or glacial moraine . . . .

COASTAL FEATURES

Rock bare or awash . . . .

Exposed wreck . . . .

Depth curve; sounding . . . .

Breakwater, pier, jetty, or wharf . . . .

Seawall . . . .

RIVERS, LAKES, AND CANALS

Intermittent stream . . . .

Perennial stream . . . .

Perennial river . . . .

Large falls; large rapids . . . .

Masonry dam . . . .

SUBMERGED AREAS AND BOGS

Marsh or swamp . . . .

The more frequently encountered symbols on U.S. topos. Their colors are as follows: control data and monuments, black; boundaries, black; roads and related features, red or black; buildings and related features, black; railroads and related features, black; contours, brown; mines and caves, black; surface features, brown; coastal features, blue or black; rivers, lakes, and canals, blue; submerged areas and bogs, blue. With few exceptions, the Canadian symbols are the same.

Part 2: The Legend

The margins of a map contain its legend. Like a fine frame around a painting, the legends around USGS topos improve and enhance the maps.

Here's the information they provide. The letters refer to labels on the map on pages 36-37.

A: Who created the map. In this case, the United States Department of the Interior's Geological Survey, and New York State's Department of Transportation.

B: The title takes its name from the quadrangle (Fishs Eddy). All states are subdivided into rectangles (quadrangles) based on lines of latitude and longitude. They are usually named for a town or prominent natural feature within the quadrangle. The state (New York) and county (Delaware) are also given.

C: The USGS categorizes maps by "series" according to how much land is covered. The most common is the 7.5-minute series. This means that each side of the map is 7.5 minutes long, or one-eighth of a degree. As you'll see later, navigators divide the world into degrees. Each degree consists of 60 minutes. A 7.5-minute-series map is 7.5 minutes of latitude high by 7.5 minutes of longitude wide. There is also a 15-minute series covering 15 minutes (one-quarter of a degree) of latitude, and 15 minutes of longitude.

D: Names of adjoining quadrangles. These are in parentheses, with one at each corner and one on each side. If the road you are following goes off the map, you know which new quadrangle to order so you can continue your journey. For example the left-hand, western border abuts against the Hancock quad.

Beneath each quad name are numbers and letters in small print. These are quad codes used by the Defense Department.

E: Each corner is marked with its latitude and longitude. On this 7.5-minute map, the corners are 7.5 minutes apart.

F: Every 2.5 minutes of latitude is marked by a fine black line along the right (eastern) and left (western) borders. Latitude in the northern hemisphere increases as you go north, toward the top of the map. Degrees are usually omitted, with only minutes and seconds shown. There are 60 seconds in a minute.

G: Every 2.5 minutes of longitude is marked by a fine black line along the top and bottom borders. Longitude in the western hemisphere increases as you go toward the left (west) side of the map. Degrees are usually omitted, with only minutes and seconds shown.

H: Lines of latitude and longitude are indicated by crosses where they would intersect.

I: There may be other fine black marks on the border with designations such as "690,000 feet." These are part of that state's plane coordinate system.

J: The fine blue lines along the borders are Universal Transverse Mercator (UTM) grid "ticks," part of an international reference system. Each is separated by one kilometer (or about five-eighths of a mile), making a handy scale.

K: This block of copy gives information about who did what, how they did it, and what sort of projection was used to make the map. This projection is polyconic. It also tells when the map was done, which is important. This one was compiled in 1963 and field-checked in 1965.

L: Revised information is always in purple. This map was edited in 1982 from aerial photographs taken in 1981. The information has not been field-checked. You've now got a good idea how up-to-date the map is.

M: Another title block with the quad's name, state, key latitude and longitude, and map series. Below are the dates of the last field-check and revisions.

N: Some maps show a key to road symbols, but rarely anything more.

O: The quadrangle location indicates its position within the state.

P: The scale. Here, one unit of measurement on the map equals 24,000 units full-sized. The USGS uses the 1:24,000 scale for most of its 7.5-minute-series. One inch equals 2,000 feet—about three-eighths of a mile. The 15-minute series maps use a scale of 1:62,500—one inch equals a mile. The third common scale for U.S. topos is 1:250,000 (one inch equals four miles), which gives you the "big picture" you need for expedition planning.

Q: The bar scales allow you to make scaled measurements of distance in miles, feet, and kilometers.

R: Contour Interval is the vertical distance (the change in elevation) between the brown contour lines. These are lines joining areas of equal height. The "National Geodetic Vertical Datum" is the reference point for all such elevations.

S: National Map Accuracy Standards: Horizontal accuracy: "Not more than ten percent of the points tested shall be in error by more than one-fiftieth of an inch." Vertical accuracy: "Not more than ten percent of the elevations tested shall be in error by more than one-half the contour interval."

T: The declination diagram shows the direction to the geographic north pole (shown by a star, pointing to the top of the globe), the magnetic north pole (MN, which is where a compass points to), and the grid north pole, GN, which we may ignore.

(Overleaf) Anyone adept at reading a USGS topo will have no trouble with a Canadian topo, and vice versa. Pages 38-39 show a 1:50,000 topo for Algonquin Provincial Park in Ontario. Features corresponding to those described above are labeled.

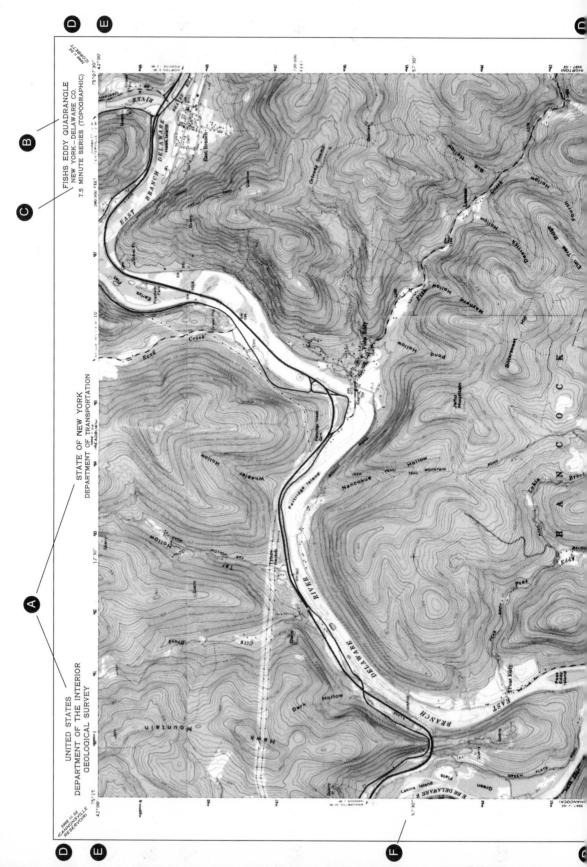

UNITED STATES
DEPARTMENT OF THE INTERIOR
GEOLOGICAL SURVEY

STATE OF NEW YORK
DEPARTMENT OF TRANSPORTATION

FISHS EDDY QUADRANGLE
NEW YORK–DELAWARE CO.
7.5 MINUTE SERIES (TOPOGRAPHIC)

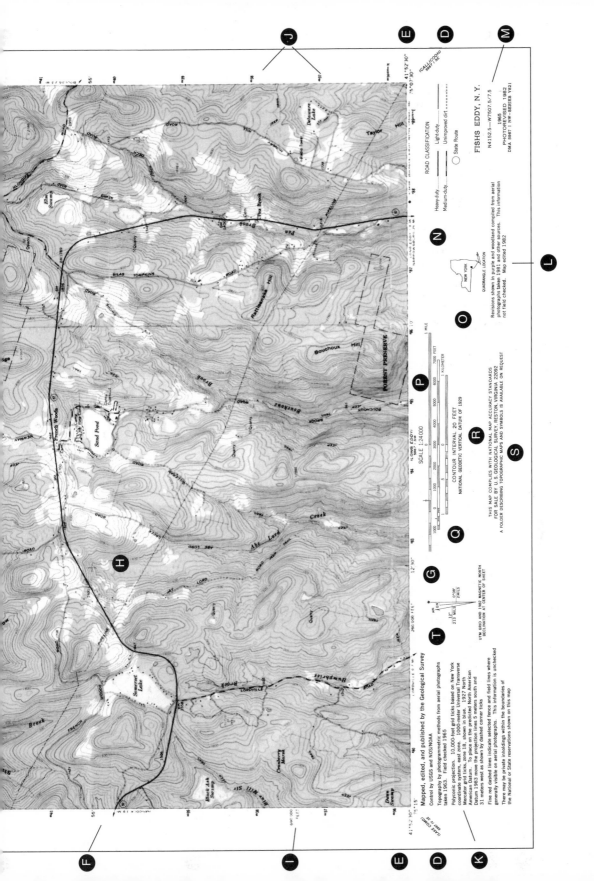

ROAD CLASSIFICATION

Heavy-duty _____ Light-duty _____

Medium-duty _____ Unimproved dirt =========

○ State Route

FISHS EDDY, N. Y.

N4152.5—W7507.5/7.5

1965

PHOTOREVISED 1982

DMA 5987 I NW—SERIES V821

Revisions shown in purple and woodland compiled from aerial
photographs taken 1981 and other sources. This information
not field checked. Map edited 1982.

QUADRANGLE LOCATION

SCALE 1:24 000

CONTOUR INTERVAL 20 FEET
NATIONAL GEODETIC VERTICAL DATUM OF 1929

THIS MAP COMPLIES WITH NATIONAL MAP ACCURACY STANDARDS
FOR SALE BY U. S. GEOLOGICAL SURVEY, RESTON, VIRGINIA 22092
A FOLDER DESCRIBING TOPOGRAPHIC MAPS AND SYMBOLS IS AVAILABLE ON REQUEST

UTM GRID AND 1982 MAGNETIC NORTH
DECLINATION AT CENTER OF SHEET

Mapped, edited, and published by the Geological Survey

Control by USGS and NOS/NOAA

Topography by photogrammetric methods from aerial photographs
taken 1963. Field checked 1965

Polyconic projection. 10,000-foot grid ticks based on New York
coordinate system, east zone. 1000-meter Universal Transverse
Mercator grid ticks, zone 18, shown in blue. 1927 North
American Datum. To place on the predicted North American
Datum 1983 move the projection lines 5 meters south and
31 meters west as shown by dashed corner ticks

Fine red dashed lines indicate selected fence and field lines where
generally visible on aerial photographs. This information is unchecked

There may be private inholdings within the boundaries of
the National or State reservations shown on this map

37

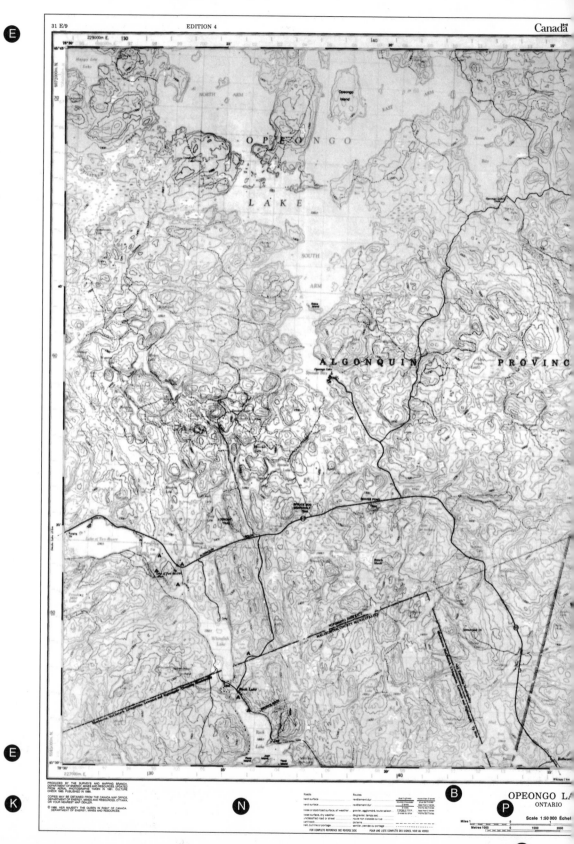

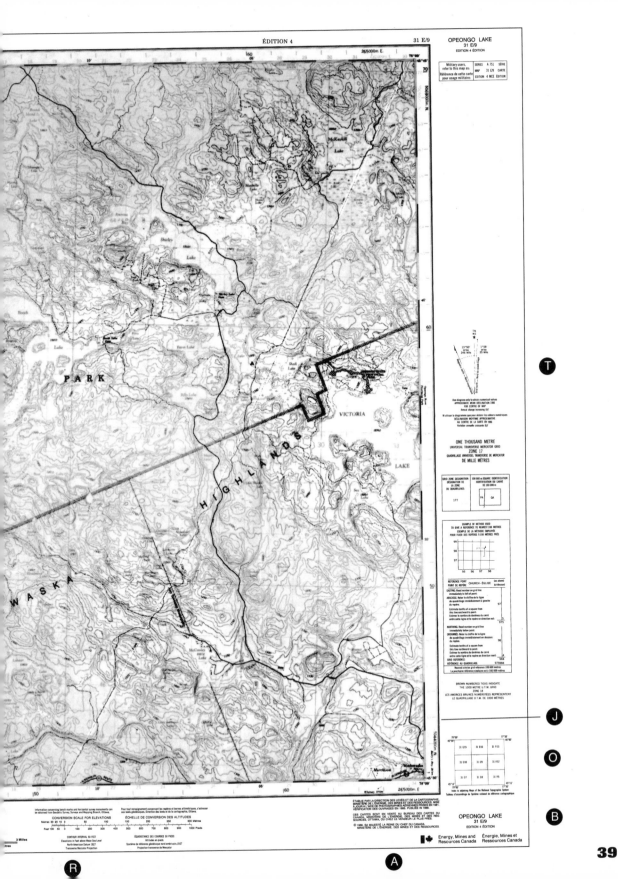

Reading the Terrain

Contour Lines: Part 1

Not even Kansas is perfectly flat. All land has undulations, dips, sinkholes, mounds, and other natural features to use as landmarks or plan our routes around. The best way to show these would be to build a scale model complete with Lilliputian-sized mountains, hills, and valleys. It would be nice, but a little hard to carry in your pocket. So mapmakers show the ups and downs of the landscape using *contour lines*. Admittedly, they're not as easy to read as a scale model, but for describing the lay of the land in two dimensions, they are remarkably effective.

The simplest designation of height on any map

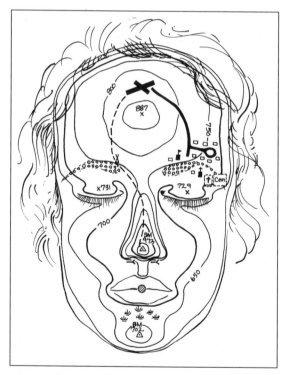

Contour lines connect points of equal elevation and can be used to describe any irregular surface. The thicker contour lines at 700 and 900 feet are contour indexes. The contour interval here is 50 feet. See page 33 for explanations of the symbols.

is an elevation, a single point with numerals beside it indicating its altitude. You'll find these marked by an × at prominent summits and at other elevation points liberally sprinkled over the map. These should not be confused with the larger + indicating where lines of latitude and longitude cross. You will also find ×s with the letters BM (for bench mark) next to them. Bench marks exist on the ground, not just on the map, usually in the form of a round metal plaque set securely in the ground for use by surveyors as a precise reference. If you stumble across a bench mark you'll know your exact latitude, longitude, and elevation.

Elevations are measured in feet or meters above a constant. Originally this was the mean (average) level of the nearest ocean, which was not always easy to determine. Now we use the "National Geodetic Vertical Datum of 1929," a preset sea level that works everywhere.

Elevations alone cannot provide an overall image of the land, of course. They are just a sporadic collection of heights. To improve upon this, mapmakers join all points of certain similar elevation in a giant connect-the-dots exercise to produce contour lines, which are marked in brown on topo maps. If a contour line is labeled 800 feet, every point on that line has an elevation above datum of 800 feet.

Sometimes contour lines occur naturally. At the shoreline of a lake, for example, the water's edge denotes points with the same elevation.

If you put together a lot of these contour lines, with each indicating a different elevation, stacking them or working them around each other, you'll have a fair depiction of the land around you. To keep such a map from getting too crowded with numbers, only every fourth or fifth contour line is labeled with its elevation. This line is a *contour index*, and is double the thickness of the other, intermediate contour lines. You may have to follow the contour index with your finger for a while to find the printed elevation, but it's always there.

All contour lines (including the contour indexes) are separated by a uniform vertical distance. Each line is an equal change of elevation from the next, and this standard interval, the *contour interval*, is noted below the bar scale in the map's margin. If the contour interval is 20 feet, consecutive contour lines will increase or decrease in height by 20 feet from their nearest neighbors. Using the contour interval, you can tell the elevation of intermediate lines. Just add or subtract the intervals to or from the closest index.

Contour intervals may change from map to map. A map of mountainous Colorado may have an interval of 100 feet, while one of the Florida Everglades might have a 10-foot interval. Cartographers choose an interval that matches the terrain. But once they choose one for a map, that's it. The contour interval will be the same for every part of that map. Only in rare cases, as when high rugged mountains meet a flat featureless plain, might this rule be broken.

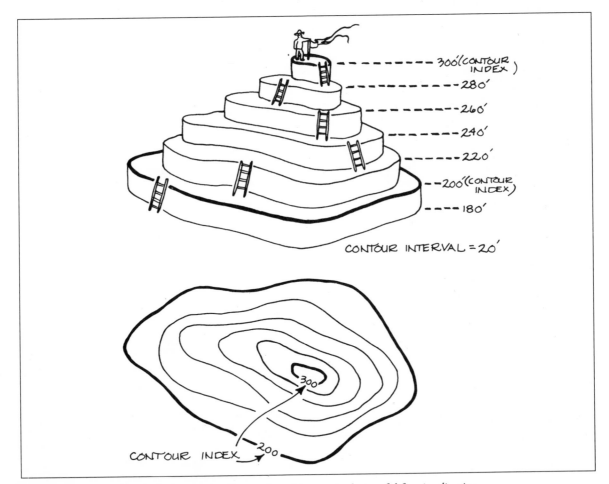

Contour lines as wedding cake layers—hardly a real-world scenario, but useful for visualization.

Contour Lines: Part 2

Ninety percent of all the contour lines on a USGS topographical map must be accurate to within at least one-half the interval. If the interval is 20 feet, only 10 percent of the lines can be as much as 10 feet from their true elevation. Taking into account the vast number of contour lines on a typical map, that's incredibly accurate.

Unfortunately, accuracy doesn't make contour lines any easier to comprehend. Interpreting contours can be a tricky visual experience. When you look at these crazy patterns of irregular lines, it's hard to believe they describe anything at all. But they do. And each of us comes to understand this in his or her own way. So, in the next few pages I'll give you a choice. See which works for you.

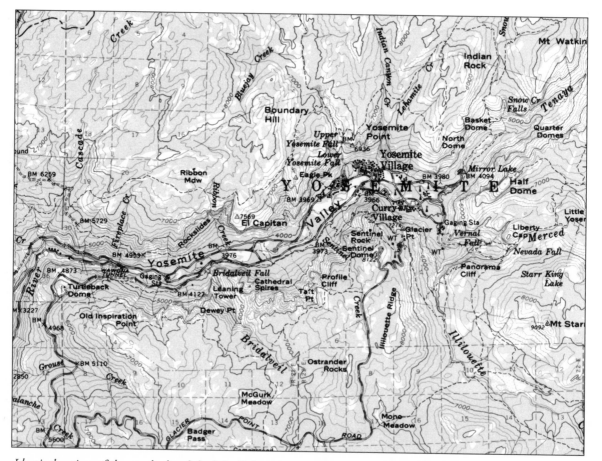

Identical sections of the standard and shaded-relief 1:125,000 scale topos of Yosemite National Park.

One of the easiest ways to get a grip on what contour lines are saying is to check your map against a similar one that has shaded relief added to it. Some topos are available in a second version of the same quad with shadows drawn in for texture. The shading gives an illusion of depth, so the contours jump out as if seen from an airplane when the sun is low in the sky. By comparing shaded and nonshaded maps of the same area, you will start to get a feel for the shape of the land and how contour lines describe this. Very few shaded relief maps are produced, because they are expensive to make and the shading reduces their usefulness as navigational tools. For interpretive use though, they can't be beaten, which is why many of the National Park Service's maps are available with shading.

Sometimes it's hard to judge whether the contours are showing a rise or a depression. In areas of uncertainty, mapmakers add hatch marks to the contour lines. These marks always point downward, at right angles (perpendicularly) to the contour line.

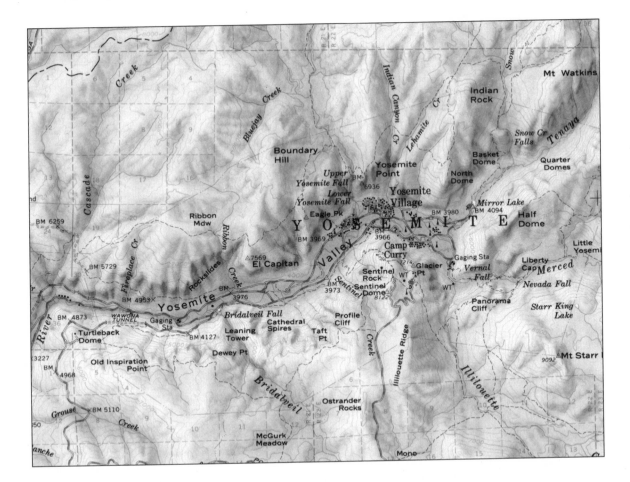

Some Rules for Interpreting Contours

- There is no beginning or end to a contour line. It is an irregularly shaped closed loop. If you could walk along a contour line you would go neither uphill nor down. You would eventually arrive at your starting point.
- The steeper the slope, the closer the spacing between lines. An extreme example of this is a vertical cliff, where contour lines fall right on top of one another on the map. The gentler the slope, and the flatter the terrain, the farther apart the lines.
- Your trail is going uphill if it regularly crosses contour lines of increasing elevation. Conversely, it's going downhill if it crosses contour lines of decreasing elevation.
- Valleys (ravines or gullies) usually show up as a series of V-shaped lines pointing toward higher ground. Sometimes the V rounds into a U if the valley is gentle.
- Ridges or spurs can be shaped like a series of V's (sharp) or U's (rounded) pointing toward lower ground.
- To determine if a group of U-shaped or V-shaped contours shows a ridge or a valley, check the elevation of contour indexes to see which way the ground is sloping, or check to see if a stream runs down the middle or side of the V's.
- A pass or saddle in a ridge has higher contour lines on each side, giving it a characteristic hourglass shape.
- Contour lines running up one side of a river or stream, crossing it, and then running back down the other side form a U or a V that points upstream. If the lines are U-shaped, the valley through which the river flows is reasonably broad and flat-bottomed. If the lines are V-shaped, the valley is fairly narrow and the ground rises steeply on each side of the river.
- A peak is depicted by the innermost ring of a near-concentric pattern of contour lines. It is often marked with an × and its elevation.

GENTLE SLOPE   MODERATE SLOPE

STEEP HILL   MOUNTAINSIDE WITH CLIFF

GULLY OR COULOIR   RIDGE

PEAK OR SUMMIT   BOWL OR CIRQUE

SADDLE, PASS, OR COL

Contour Lines: Part 3

Test your topoliteracy by matching the topo views to the appropriate profiles. (Answers on page 46.)

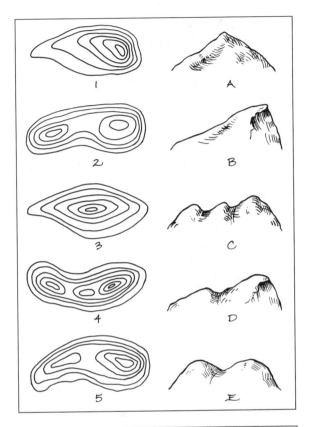

Four views of a mountain. A familiar landmark can look very different when viewed from an unfamiliar perspective.

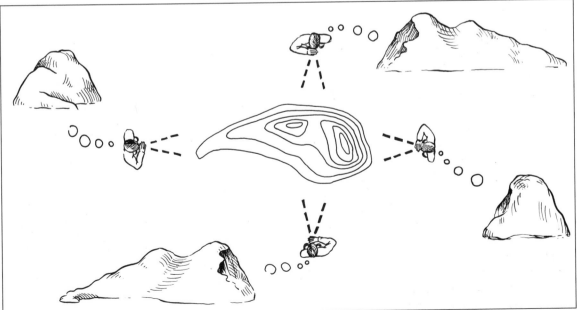

What the Lines Don't Tell You

Topographical maps impart a lot of information, but they can't tell you everything. To really see what the map is trying to reveal, you have to learn to read between the lines. And sometimes it's what's between those lines that matters most. Contour lines can't describe every feature. For example, the contour interval might cause lines to run slightly above and below a significant detail such as a dip or a rise. So the map won't tell you it's there.

The greater the contour interval, the greater the chance of missing something important. Very often this can't be helped. Intervals may need to be widely spaced in mountainous regions—50 feet apart or more—to avoid having too many lines crowding the map and making it illegible. It is not unheard of that a 40-foot cliff fails to show up on such a map. You might be traversing what you expect to be an easy slope when suddenly a cliff appears out of nowhere, stopping your progress and making you wonder if you're on the right trail.

Just because something isn't shown on the map doesn't necessarily mean it doesn't exist. You have to interpret the character of the landscape as well as the map that depicts it.

Index lines, too, can be misleading. Since they are darker and more pronounced, we often tend to focus exclusively on them, ignoring the less conspicuous intermediate lines. A quick glance resulting from haste or plain laziness will give you a mental image of the landscape gathered from only the darker lines and depicting only the coarsest features. Take your time. Study all the lines, lest useful information go wasted.

Through no fault of the cartographer or you, some things are impossible to infer from even the finest of maps. For instance, there's no knowing whether closely grouped contour lines mean an impassable, rock-strewn cliff or a smooth slope up which you could scramble. Some things you can't know until you get there, so try to leave yourself options and backup routes along the way.

Last, consider your perspective and elevation when interpreting a map. Are you higher or lower than the surrounding terrain? Maps show the whole spectrum of heights from the lowest valley floor to the highest summit, and you may not be able to take all this in from where you are. That series of ridges shown on the map may be those low hills way below you.

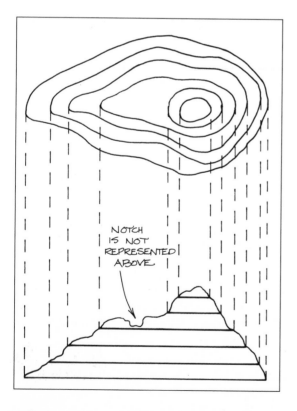

NOTCH IS NOT REPRESENTED ABOVE.

Reading the Terrain

Slope Profiles

A map's contour lines give the impression of a world built like a wedding cake, layer upon layer, with sharp vertical rises or descents (the contour interval) between the steps. Thankfully, things aren't like that. Between the lines are slopes of varying steepness. The severity of a slope is expressed as a gradient—the relationship between the contour interval and the horizontal distance between contour lines—which tells you how steep or flat the land is. It's a very important factor when deciding your route.

For the irregular terrain you would probably encounter over a long day's walk, it would be useful to know what gradients to expect. This would give you an idea of the trail's difficulty and what to look for along the way.

The best way to do this is to construct a slope profile—a scaled-down cross-section of the land. It's as if a vertical slice had been cut out along the trail line. Before you set out, try making one. With reference to the numbered steps in the illustration on page 48, here's how:

1: Mark your trail on the map.
2: On a piece of clean paper, construct a grid for the slope profile, as follows. (Use the scale on the map for all measurements on your grid.)

    Draw a horizontal line slightly longer than the length of your trail on the map, and label it with the elevation of the lowest contour line your trail crosses. This will be your baseline.

    Draw a series of horizontal lines parallel to the baseline using the contour interval (found on the map) to set the spacing between the lines. If the contour interval produces grid lines that are too tightly spaced for convenience, use every other contour line or only the ones that show significant changes in elevation. Work upward until you have drawn the highest contour line your trail crosses. Make sure the eleva-

tion of each contour line (horizontal line on your grid) has been indicated. Your grid is now complete.

3: Gather horizontal distances and elevations along the trail by making a straightedge from a piece of paper. Put a mark at one end of the straightedge. Write "Start" and the elevation of the beginning of your trail next to it. Place the mark where your trail starts on the map. Using the mark as a pivot point, turn the straightedge until it crosses the next intersection of your trail with a contour line. Put a mark on the straightedge and write down the elevation of that contour. Use the new mark as a pivot point and turn the paper to meet the next intersection of your trail and a contour line.
    Keep adding marks and elevations along the straightedge until you reach the end of the trail. Mark that as "End," with its elevation next to it.
4: To transfer the horizontal distances and elevations from the straightedge to the grid, lay the straightedge along the grid baseline. Project vertical lines upward from the marks on the straightedge to meet their corresponding horizontal contour lines. For example, if a mark says 600 feet, project upward until you reach the 600-foot contour line and make a small X. Do this for all the marks, including "Start" and "End."
5: Connect the X's with a smooth line to make the slope profile.

Your slope profile gives you an indication of the comparative steepness of various legs of your trail. The actual profile you obtain is governed by the spacing of the lines on the grid and is not intended to represent the steepness of the ground. Experience will soon enable you to gauge the difficulty of a trail from the number of feet it rises in a certain distance.

see illustration
next page

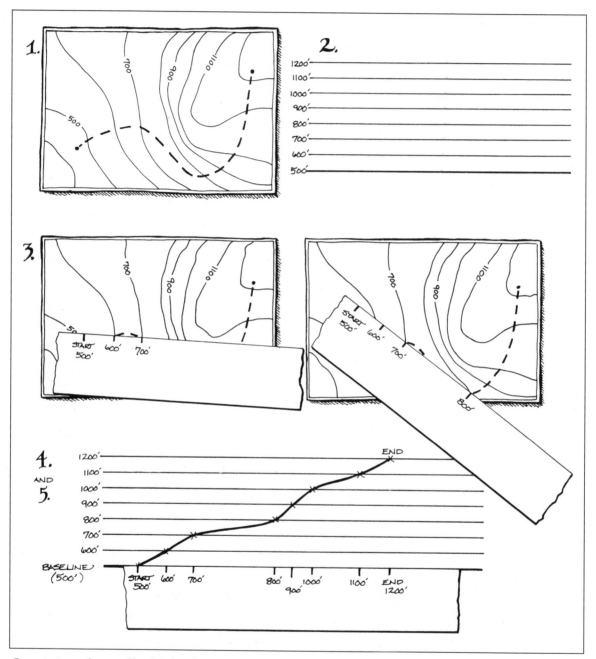

Constructing a slope profile. Numbered steps correspond to numbered paragraphs on page 47.

Slope Gradients

When there is a single slope ahead of you, or only one that is of any importance, it will be a lot easier to describe it numerically than to go through the rigmarole of drafting a complete slope profile. Besides, trying to draw a profile while on the trail is often impractical. Instead, we can come up with some numbers to give us a sense of how steep the slope is.

As an example, say you are starting to hike along a trail toward a summit and want to know how difficult the walk ahead will be.

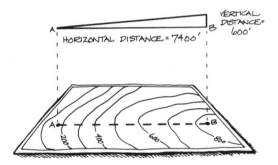

Since a gradient compares vertical and horizontal distances, we need to know:

1: The change in elevation, which is the vertical distance; and
2: The length of the trail, which is the horizontal distance.

You get the vertical distance by counting contour lines; in our example it is 600 feet. Horizontal distance is measured using the map's scale, and in this case it's 7,400 feet, or about 1.4 miles.

Using this, we can get a ratio that shows how much the trail rises (or falls). By dividing the horizontal distance (7,400 feet) by the vertical distance (600 feet) we get 12 feet. The trail's gradient rises 1 foot for every 12 feet traveled horizontally. The gradient is therefore 1 in 12. The smaller the second number, the steeper the grade.

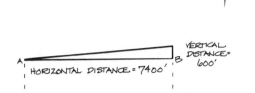

Another ratio states the same thing in a different way. This time, divide the vertical distance in feet (600) by the horizontal distance in miles (1.4). The answer is 429. This means that for every mile you walk horizontally, you climb 429 feet.

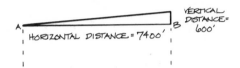

Gradient can also be expressed as a percentage of an angle. Dead flat would be 0 percent, while a mile's climb in a mile of horizontal distance would be 100%. To find the percentage gradient, divide the vertical distance in feet (600) by the horizontal distance in feet (7,400). You'll get .08, or an 8 percent gradient. An easy walk.

$$\frac{\text{VERTICAL DISTANCE}}{\text{HORIZONTAL DISTANCE}} = \frac{600'}{7400'} = .08$$
$$\text{GRADIENT} = 8\%$$

Here's what this means. A gradient of 100 percent, or 45 degrees, will probably have you scrambling on all fours. A gradient of 40 percent is impassable to vehicles. A jeep's practical limit is about 25 percent, which is hard walking, but acceptable. An elevation change of 1,000 feet in a mile will generate a good sweat.

Journey over all the universe in a map, without the expense and fatigue of traveling, without suffering the inconveniences of heat, cold, hunger, and thirst.

—Don Quixote de la Mancha
Miguel de Cervantes

49

Latitude and Longitude

We have overlaid the earth with an imaginary grid made from lines of latitude and longitude—an immense pattern of avenues and cross-streets, with each intersection precisely defining a location. Lines of latitude run horizontally, east and west, and lie parallel to one another, to be used as a scale for measuring distances north and south of the equator. The equator, the earth's waistband, is at 0 degrees latitude. The north pole and the south pole are at 90 degrees latitude. So latitudes increase as they approach the poles. If your house were in Albuquerque, it would be near the 35th parallel north of the equator. Buenos Aires lies near the 35th parallel south of the equator. Latitude is always expressed in degrees north or south (of the equator).

Lines of longitude run vertically, north and south, but are not parallel. They are spread out around the equator and come together at the poles. They're used as a scale for measuring distances east and west of Greenwich, England. Why there? Since there is no north/south line comparable to the equator, the British took the initiative toward the end of the 17th century and created an artificial line that passed through Greenwich Observatory, just outside London.

This line is 0 degrees longitude, and all other lines of longitude, or meridians, are measured in degrees east or west of it. Your home in Albuquerque is close to 107 degrees west. If you lived in Hanoi, you'd be close to 107 degrees east. Longitude is always expressed in degrees east or west (of Greenwich).

Because degrees of longitude are numbered similarly both east and west of Greenwich, the numbers meet on the opposite side of the world at longitude 180, known as the International Date Line.

A degree (1°) is divided into 60 minutes (60'), and a minute is divided into 60 seconds (60"). When describing a position, latitude, by convention, is stated first—as being north or south. Longitude is either east or west. So your home in Albuquerque might be accurately located at 35° 14' 27" N, 106° 43' 13" W.

USGS topo maps do not show full lines of lati-

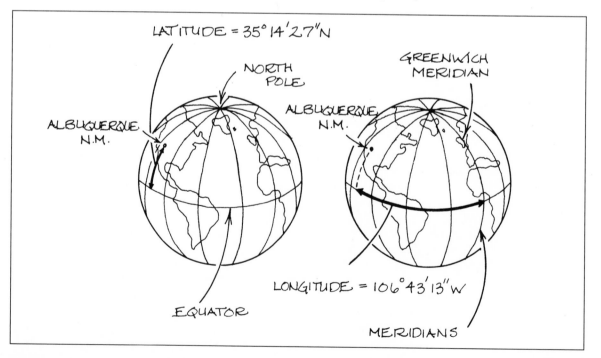

tude and longitude, only marks on the borders and crosses on the map where the lines meet, at intervals of 2.5 minutes (written as 2.5' or 2' 30"). To identify a position, draw your own lines to join the marks or crosses. Then draw lines parallel to them from the point you want to identify, out to the borders. Latitude and longitude are then found by interpolating where the lines fall between the marks.

Because lines of longitude converge as they get closer to the poles, the north border of a 7.5-minute map (each side being 7.5 minutes long) is slightly shorter than its south border. This is why maps are called quadrangles (four angles) rather than rectangles or squares (four right angles). This convergence is very slight over the comparatively tiny area covered by the average topo map, so for all practical purposes such lines of longitude can be regarded as being parallel.

Incidentally, a degree of latitude is a handy unit of measurement, equalling 69 statute miles (round it up to 70), or 1.15 miles for a minute. Therefore the north and south borders on a 7.5-minute map are separated by 8.625 miles.

But don't try to measure distances with degrees of longitude. While degrees of latitude and longitude are the same length on the equator, that's not true anywhere else. In New York (40 degrees north), convergence causes a degree of longitude to be 53 miles long. At the Arctic Circle (66.5 degrees north), it's only about 27 miles.

So, if you're using degrees and minutes to find distance on a north-facing map at the rate of 69 statute miles to the degree, always use the latitude scales on the left and right sides, never the longitude scales at top and bottom.

The same applies to a nautical chart, on which one degree of latitude equals exactly 60 nautical miles, and one minute equals exactly one mile. How lucky for sailors.

I am a firm believer in doing virtually all navigating with just a map. As long as you can see features around you and relate them to the map, you know where you are. The easiest way to do this is by setting, or orienting, the map; this involves turning the map until the features you can see are in their correct positions relative to where you are. If you walk with the map set, it is easier to relate visible features to it.

—The Backpacker's Handbook
Chris Townsend
Ragged Mountain Press, 1993

Scale

Maps are reality reduced to manageable size, with every detail uniformly proportioned to what it represents. The map's scale, or degree of reduction, is noted along its bottom border.

Scale is most often expressed as a ratio. A scale of 1:24,000 means that one inch on the map represents 24,000 inches in the real world. Another way of looking at the ratio is as if it were a fraction. For example, a scale of 1:24,000 means that what is shown on the map is 1/24,000th its actual size. Both ratios and fractions demonstrate how much smaller the map is than the area it represents.

You'll often hear the confusing terms *large scale* and *small scale* applied to maps. Confusing because they mean the opposite of what it seems they should. A scale of 1:20,000 is larger than one of 1:50,000 because 1/20,000 is a larger part of the whole than 1/50,000. Even though 50,000 is the larger number, it makes a smaller ratio or fraction, just as one-half is larger than one-quarter.

All you need to know is this: The bigger the second number, the smaller the scale. The smaller the second number, the larger the scale.

Why choose a map with a larger or smaller scale? Well, small-scale maps cover a large area, so the details on them are small. Large-scale maps cover a small area, so the details show up larger.

Here's an easy way to remember:

Small scale = small detail.
Large scale = large detail.

A small-scale map would be good for planning a long trip and getting an overview of the lay of the land. A large-scale map would be best for precise navigation and picking out landmarks en route.

For convenience, scales on topographical maps are calculated to make it easy to measure map distances with a ruler in inches or centimeters. Typical scales are:

- 1:24,000. A large scale encompassing a small area in great detail. May cover only 70 square miles or less. Found on most 7.5-minute-series topos. 1" = 2,000'. (That's 2.64 inches to the mile.)

1:24,000

South Tarryall Peak in Pike National Forest, Colorado, as shown in 1:24,000, 1:100,000 and 1:250,000 scale topos.

- 1:25,000. Similar to the above, but easier to use with the metric system. 1 cm = 250 m. 1" = 2,083'.
- 1:62,500. A practical, all-purpose scale for wilderness travel. Found on most 15-minute series topos. 1" = 1 mile (approx.).

- 1:250,000 Used for small-scale mapping of large areas. Provides a very generalized feeling of the landscape. May cover 100 linear miles or more. 1" = 4 miles (approx.).

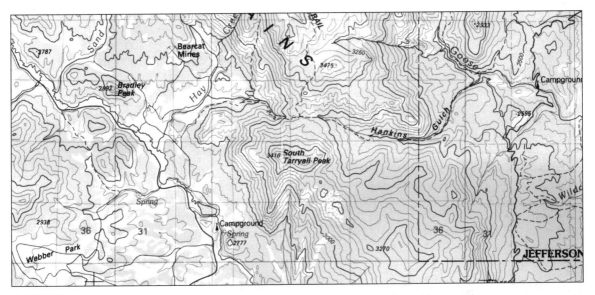

1:100,000

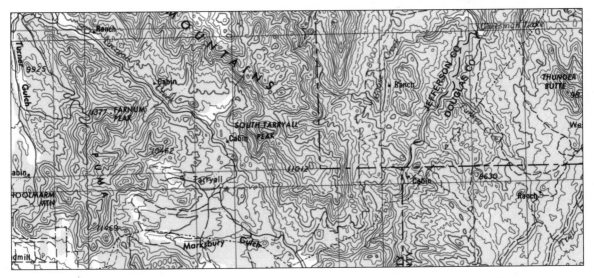

1:250,000

Distance

To measure distance, we use the graphic bar scale in the map's legend, usually found in the lower margin of USGS topos. The easiest way to do this is by marking off the distance on the edge of a piece of paper and transferring it to the bar scale.

Bar scales read both ways from 0. To the right of 0 are whole numbers. To the left are the finer divisions. Lay the paper's edge along the bar scale with the right-hand mark on a whole number. Read off the left-hand mark for the fractional measurements. In the example below, the distance measured is 4,400 feet.

You can also measure distances with a ruler or the graduated baseplate of some orienteering compasses. By knowing how much an inch (or centimeter) represents, you can make good estimations of distance.

Such methods are satisfactory when you can go directly from one point to another. But that will be the exception, because, as the saying goes, "There are no straight lines in nature." To measure the length of a river, or the meanderings of a trail, we need something that's flexible—such as dental floss, string, the lanyard from your compass, a pipe cleaner, or a wire twist-seal. Place one end at your starting point, follow the route, and mark where you finish with your thumbnail or a sharp kink (in wire). Straighten, place it next to the bar scale without stretching it, and read the distance.

You can also use the edge of a piece of paper to do the same thing by dividing the route up into a series of short, straight segments. A word of advice, though: Don't bother with one of those map-measuring gadgets with a little wheel. They work only if the map is absolutely flat and has never been folded—both of which are highly unlikely in the field.

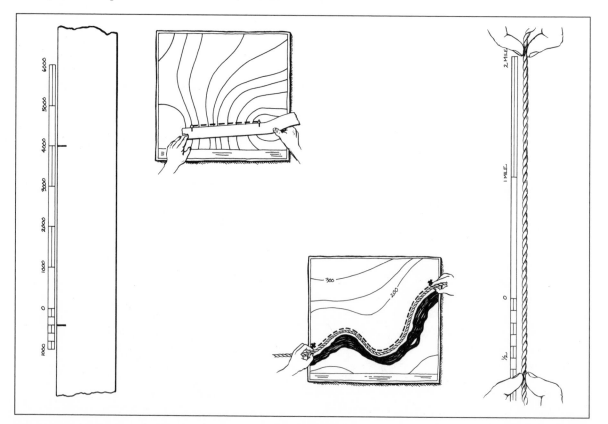

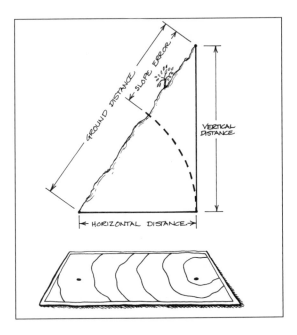

Maps show distance as if the world's surface were flat, which it isn't, and can lead you into underestimating how far you might have to travel. There's a big difference between uphill (or downhill) miles and level ones, and the steeper the slope's gradient, the greater the difference becomes. This is called slope error, the discrepancy between actual ground distances and measured map distances.

There's no easy method of computing slope error, especially on uneven surfaces. The best you can do is be aware of the severity of the gradients and changes in elevations, and know that your route will be longer (and harder to walk) than shown on the map.

Direction

What It Is

Wherever you stand, you have a great choice of directions toward which to face. If all those choices were joined together, they would make a "circle of directions" around you. For the sake of convenience we'll divide this circle into 360 parts and call each part a degree. We'll start at 0 degrees and go around clockwise (the direction of the sun) to 360 degrees, so you can describe where you are facing at any time.

But where on the circle would we start? Where would we put the 0? The logical place would be a spot that never moves. It would be a constant, a point of reference. And, to make it handy, this point of reference should always be easy to find, either with our eyes or some reliable gadget that would always guide us toward it. Luckily we have such a point of reference. We call it the north pole.

In ancient times, someone noticed that one star—it may have been Draconis then and not Polaris—never moved in relation to the spinning earth. It was a constant, and a much more accurate and better reference point than the ever-moving places where the sun rises (toward the east) or

sets (toward the west). So they adopted the star in the north as a special reference.

Then came the compass, which made north easier to find at all times of day and in all weather. With 0 degrees at north, everything else on the circle falls into place, regardless of how you turn. With this universal reference, you can now indicate a specific direction and be able to describe it to others.

We start with the four cardinal points: north (which is 0 degrees and also 360 degrees), east (90 degrees), south (halfway around at 180 degrees), and west (270 degrees). There are also four intercardinal points: northeast, southeast, southwest, and northwest. These can be even further divided into points such as south-southeast. But these finer designations are rarely inscribed on most compasses, or anything else indicating directions. You'll generally see only N, E, S, W, and the numerical degrees in between.

This north-referring system would be perfect if it weren't for one problem—there is not just one north, there are two, and on some maps even three!

No doubt you've heard that a compass always points to the north pole. Well, that's not quite correct. The earth has two north poles: the geographic, or true, north pole, which is at one end of the earth's axis of rotation; and the magnetic north pole, which is at the northern end of the planet's magnetic core. While geographic, or true, north is in a fixed position on top of the world, magnetic north is slowly wobbling about somewhere to the west of Baffin Island, Canada.

A compass points to magnetic north, not geographic north, and the angular difference between these two varies with your position on earth. This angle is called *declination* on land maps. On nautical charts, however, it's called *variation*, because in astronavigation the term declination is reserved for the angular distance of a heavenly body north or south of the celestial equator. We'll learn a lot more about declination in the next chapter. Meanwhile, if you look at a map's legend you'll find a declination diagram, which shows the magnitude of this angular difference in the particular area mapped.

The long vertical line, the one with the star at its

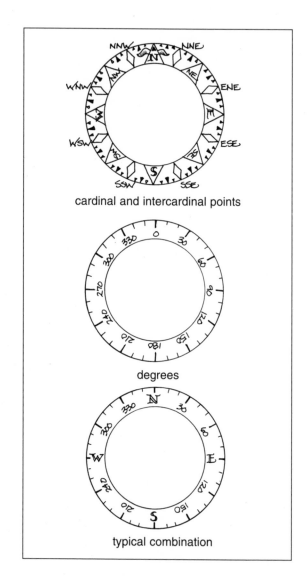

cardinal and intercardinal points

degrees

typical combination

end, points to geographic (true) north. This is the reference line cartographers use, and the one you should use when finding your way with only a map.

The second-longest line, the one with an arrow and "MN" at its tip, points to magnetic north. When finding your way with a compass, this is the north you will usually use. Notice the "12 degrees" and "213 MILS"? These are notations for the amount of magnetic declination in this area. A mil is a unit of angular measurement that divides a circle into 6,400 increments for

those (like military gunners) who need greater precision. Luckily, we can safely ignore mils.

The shortest line, marked GN, stands for grid north. Grid is short for the Universal Transverse Mercator Grid, which cartographers use to reduce the distortion induced by the earth's curvature upon a flat map. Don't worry about it. It's of no use to us.

A word of warning about declination diagrams: Only the geographic north line is always aligned properly. The others may or may not be drawn at the correct angles. This is especially so with smaller angles which would not show up, and are therefore exaggerated to make the differences clear. Be advised also that because the magnetic north pole wanders, the local declination will change with time, albeit predictably. Though the rate of change is not great—typically ½ to 1 degree every five years depending on where you are—it can add up. We'll return to this point in Chapter 3.

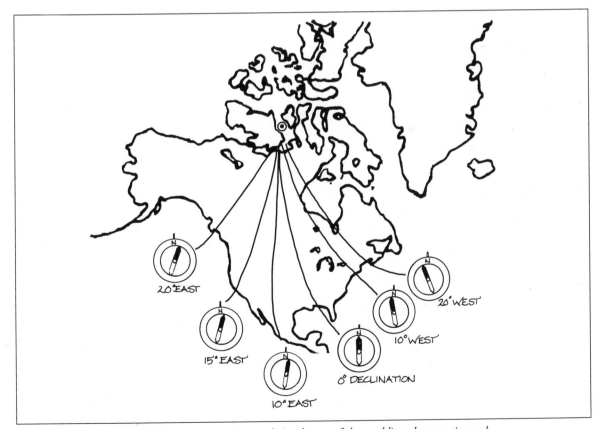

Declination is the difference between geographic north (at the top of the world) and magnetic north (the place your compass points to).

Direction

How to Measure It

On almost all maps, when the printing is right side up, geographic north will be at the top. This enables you to find the four cardinal points with great ease. But what about the other 356 degrees? How do you find them?

Here's how. Let's say you have marked your position on a map and want to find the direction to somewhere else, such as the top of a far-off hill. To do this, you'll need a pencil, a straight-edge (a ruler, an edge of the map flopped over on itself, or a folded piece of paper), and a cheap plastic protractor.

1: Begin by drawing lines of latitude and longitude, using the marks on the borders and crosses on the map. You now have north/south and east/west reference lines to use for this and future problems.

2: From your marked position, draw a straight line (your course line) through the hill's summit until it intersects a reference line (such as a line of latitude, longitude, or any one of the map's borders).

3: Place the base of the protractor (the 0- to 180-degree line) on the reference line, and its center over your direction line.

4: Read the number of degrees off the protractor to give you the angle between the reference line and your course line. This may provide your direction right away, or you may need to use some simple arithmetic.

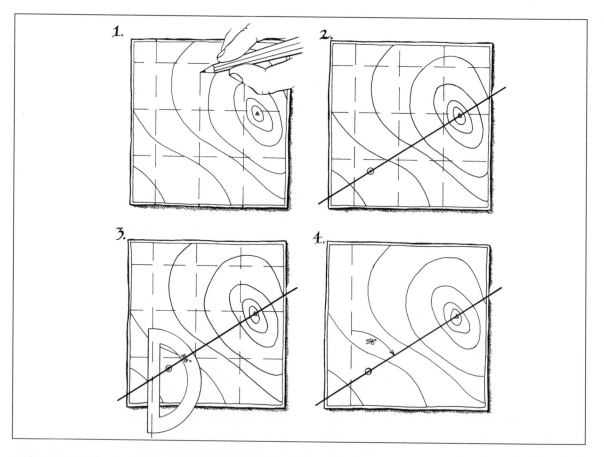

Putting Yourself on the Map

Finding Your Position

If, as we've said before, a map is reduced reality, then by envisioning ourselves brought down to scale (at 1:24,000 you'd be about .003" tall) we can walk through both worlds—the real one and the map's—at the same time. As we pick out landmarks in one, we can relate it to the other, thus keeping track of our ever-changing position.

To do this, start by identifying your initial location on the map, a single spot. Once this is done you then have to orient (align) the map to the surrounding world to maintain the illusion of map and reality being as one.

First let's find out where you are, then follow with how to orient the map.

To locate your starting position, and any spot thereafter, you can use one of two methods on the map.

1: Landmarks. If you are standing at an obvious and well-defined location you'll know where you are on the map. This could be a building, the foot of a bridge, a benchmark at a summit, a fire tower, a sign, the spot where a road ends, a waterfall, or anything else that is unique and can be matched to a symbol on the map.

2: Crossed reference lines. A reference line is an easily identifiable elongated feature. If you're standing near a road, trail, river, tree line, railroad track, shoreline, overhead power line, backbone of a ridge, or the base of a narrow valley, you're next to a reference line. A good reference line is recognizable enough to stand out from the surrounding landscape and is clearly indicated on the map.

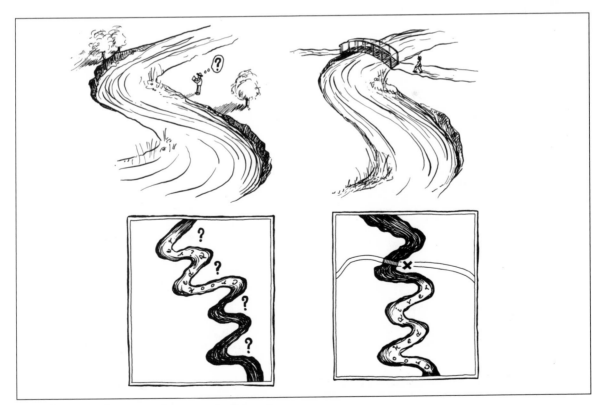

Right diagram is the position from crossed reference lines.

Once you find your reference line on the map you can say with assurance that you are somewhere on it. You just won't know where. This may not sound like a good way of finding out where you are, but it does eliminate everything else in the world except that one line—which is quite a bit of real estate.

To make that reference line into a single identifiable spot you must cross it with another reference line. Let's say you're on Mediterranean Avenue. That's your reference line. But where on Mediterranean? After a short walk you come to an intersection. It's Boardwalk, another reference line. Where the two cross makes a point, or a fix (because it fixes your position). Your position is now pinpointed, and that is the only place where you could be.

Other fixes could be from where a trail fords a river, a railroad crossing, a ridge ending in a cliff, a fork in a road, or where a road meets a lake's

shore. If you look carefully there are crossed reference lines everywhere.

You can also create a reference line from a transit or range. When two objects appear to overlap with one behind the other, putting themselves into alignment from your point of view, they form a range. If you draw a line on the map connecting the two objects you would be somewhere on it.

Orienting the Map

To successfully use a map as a direction-finding tool you'll have to correlate it to the world it represents. Luckily it is very easy to orient a map—all you have to do is look around and align the map with the surrounding landscape. Once this relationship is established you can plan routes and explore with confidence. Begin by looking for easily identifiable features like peaks, clearings, buildings, and roads that are also on the map. Compare what you see to what is on the map, turning the map until it relates to what you see. If something is ahead of you, it should be ahead of your position on the map. If something is to your right, it should be to the right of your position on the map. Once this is done, you're oriented. By keeping the map oriented as you travel, with the direction of travel forward, it will be easier to relate what you see to what is on the map, and reduce the risk of getting lost. Orienting the map will also give you an approximate idea of your location, although not as accurately as with a landmark or crossed lines of reference.

The only problem with keeping a map oriented is that you might wind up holding it at an angle or even upside down, making it difficult to read names, notes, or symbols. So some folks hold their maps right side up (north on top) regardless of the direction they are facing. This can take a lot of visual juggling because when heading south, for example, anything to your left on the map is actually to your right. Interpreting the world in reverse can be very disorienting, but some people can and prefer to do it. In general, orienting the map is the better and more reliable method,

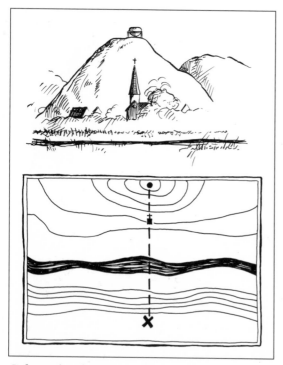

Reference line from a transit or range.

allowing you to determine directions directly.

There may be times when it is impossible to orient a map by observation alone, such as when you're in a deep wood, on a barren plain, or in any landscape devoid of mapped features. Sometimes too many features can be just as bad. If you are surrounded by endless hills, it might be impossible to tell one from another. In any of these cases the only way to orient the map and yourself will be with a compass, which we'll discuss in Chapter 3.

Orienting Yourself

Once you've got the map oriented so it matches the land, you can . . .

Identify unknown landmarks.

With the map oriented put one end of a straightedge, like a pencil or stick, on your known position. Turn the straightedge until it points to the landmark in the field that you want to identify. Now study the map where the straightedge lies. The unknown landmark will be on that line. Find it by matching features such as elevation, foliage, shapes, and distance from your position.

Find your approximate location.

If you are not near any mapped landmarks or crossed lines of references you can get a rough

approximation of your position by *triangulation*.

With the map oriented, find at least two (three is even better) distant landmarks that are also on the map. Put the center of a straightedge, like a pencil or stick, across the spot marking one of the landmarks. Turn the straightedge until one end points to the actual landmark. When this is done the opposite end will point toward your position. Draw a long line in that direction. Do the same with the other landmarks, and where the lines meet will be your approximate position.

It will be best to do this with the map on the ground, rather than in your hands. Don't be fooled by lines meeting at one nice, neat point. This technique is only a rough, although very useful, way of finding an approximate position (we'll do it by compass with considerably more accuracy later). Check the landscape around you to see if the point where the lines meet makes sense.

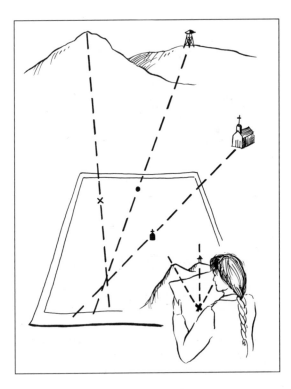

Map Care and Gear

Good topo maps are relatively inexpensive, so it's easy to think of them as expendable. And they are, if you're near a store where they can be replaced. But in the wilds this won't be possible: Take care of your maps.

Folding

One of the best ways to extend a map's life is to fold it. A properly folded map stays out of harm's way in pocket or pack, is simple to refold without resorting to origami, and is convenient to use in high winds. The method shown is an adaptation of the classic commuter's newspaper-fold. It makes a compact package that lets you look at any part of the map without having to open it all the way. Fold lines are parallel to the borders, making it easy to pick out the cardinal directions.

Protection

If you're going to be out in foul weather or in a boat, you might want to apply a water-repellent coating. That's water repellent, not waterproof—which can only be done by lamination. This is expensive and makes the map almost impossible to fold.

A water-resistant coating can be applied with spray-on lacquers or acrylics found at art supply stores. Spray both sides in a series of light coats rather than one heavy coat, which may give you blobs of glop that add to the topography. Specialty map stores carry sprays or liquids specifically made for the job, usually costing more than the map they are to protect. These shops may also have map pouches in leather, canvas, or plastic. Keeping your map in a protective cover prevents the folds from wearing and corners from curling over. But most store-bought ones are unnecessarily bulky. By far the best (and cheapest) protection is a sealable baggie. And when yours gets too beat up, you can use it to hold your lunch.

Paraphernalia

- Keep your chosen route from getting lost in a tangle of contour lines by using a yellow highlighter felt-tip pen to make the route stand out at a glance. Bring along a stub of a pencil with its eraser still intact, and a knife (always good idea anyway) to give it a fine point.
- A pocket magnifying glass will help clarify information printed in tiny "mouse type" and count densely crowded contour lines.
- A plastic (so it won't effect a compass) ruler will give you a straightedge for drawing and a way to measure scaled distances. If there's room, carry a 12-inch ruler; if not, a 6-inch one will do.
- The millimeter side of the ruler can be useful even if you're not into metric. Forget that they're millimeters. Just think of those closely spaced, logically numbered, easy-to-count, marks as a general measuring tool. Isn't it easier to read the map distance between two points as 38 "somethings" rather than 1 and $^{13}/_{16}$th inches? You can also use the millimeter marks to interpolate between indicated lines of latitude and longitude.
- Finally, you'll need a cheap clear-plastic grade school protractor to show directions in degrees. If you have the room, a semicircular one with a 6-inch rule on the bottom will do double service.
- When choosing navigational equipment go low-tech, replaceable, affordable, rugged, and reliable.

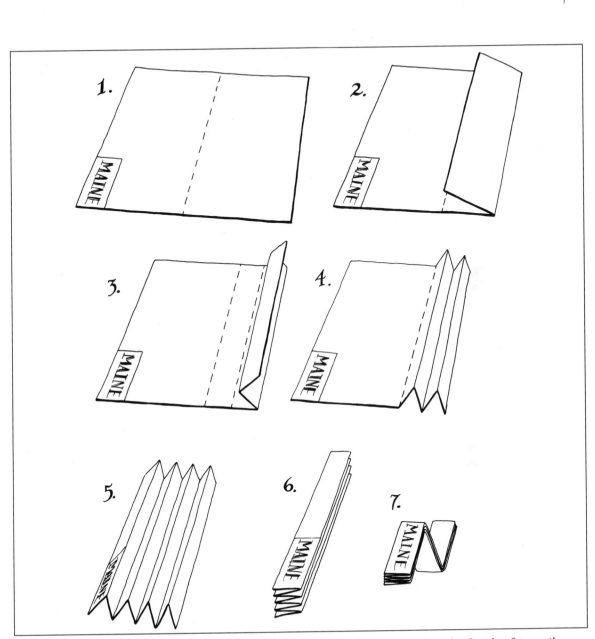

Folding a topo. Start with the title block in the lower left-hand corner. Rub the folds down hard with a fingernail to make sharp creases. Finish with the title block on top.

Chapter Three

COMPASSES

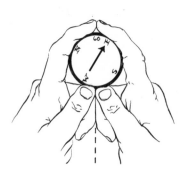

There aren't many things in this world that you can trust implicitly, but a compass is one of them. Few man-made objects are more worthy of your confidence. Of course the compass does have its idiosyncrasies, but once understood, it's one of the most reliable pieces of hardware you'll ever acquire. It won't let you down.

The golden rule is this: When you're confused and disoriented, trust your compass.

Perversely, this seems just what we are least likely to do when lost, preferring to defer to that creature of fiction—our sense of direction. A not-uncommon phrase heard from those recently rescued is that when they consulted their compass, "There seemed to be something wrong with the damn thing." There hardly ever is.

But it's hard to have confidence in a primitive gadget and the unseen force of magnetism. Although you might, in principle, be willing to suspend your suspicions while reading this in the warm comfort of your living room, would you be able to do so out on the trail, when everything looks like everything else, and nothing looks as it should?

Well, if you're going to be a successful navigator you'll have to make this leap of faith. You must learn to trust your compass, and to let go of your preconceptions. Don't be afraid to alter your mental map.

The following pages explain how compasses work, what they are capable of doing, their limitations, and their quirks. Once you've read this, you really should head outdoors and prove to yourself that you can trust your compass. Confidence comes only with practice.

Later in this chapter is a section on the types of compasses. Pick one you think might suit you, then buy an inexpensive model. Experiment until you feel comfortable and secure with this wonderfully simple—yet unfailingly trustworthy—piece of magic.

What Compasses Can Do

Most of us have owned a compass, and many of us have been lost at least once while carrying one. Merely being able to find north won't, by itself, keep you from getting lost. You have to keep track of north (and therefore south, east, and west) from the very start of, and all through, your journey. A compass shows only directions, not position.

As discussed in Chapter 1, one of the basic requirements for not getting lost is always to maintain a constant reference point or line you can relate to. Without that you have nothing to work from, nothing of substance on which to base your choice of directions. A compass, by always pointing north (and south), will give you that reference. If you start with and maintain that reference, here are some of the things a compass can do for you:

- By checking the compass to find your intended direction of travel when first heading out, you'll be able to tell later (when you're not quite sure of things) whether you're coming or going.
- A compass will keep you pointed in the right direction in the absence of a trail or markers.
- If you know your general direction of travel, a compass can help you make the right choice at a fork in the trail.
- We tend to veer to one side as we walk, but a compass will keep you headed in a straight line.
- A compass can help you walk toward something you can't see because it's either too far off or obscured by trees, fog, snow, or darkness.
- When you deviate from your direct course to get around an obstruction, a compass will help (only help) get you back on track toward your destination.
- If you walk a direct compass course to somewhere, you can return by following that course in reverse.
- You can return to your starting point even if you followed no fixed outward route by

In the North, where lakes can be huge, sprawling, confusing, elaborately sprinkled with islands, bays, and points, and surrounded by low-relief land with few prominent landmarks, you must navigate carefully. You will need a good compass and the knowledge to use it. In addition to compass skills, you will need to develop map and correlation skills.

—A Snow Walker's Companion
Garrett and Alexandra Conover
Ragged Mountain Press, 1994

keeping track of each change of direction and distance traveled.
- A compass will get you back to a line of reference, like a road or river, after you've been wandering haphazardly.
- You can return to a spot by noting compass directions, or bearings, to landmarks around it. If, when you return, the compass directions to all the landmarks are the same— you have found that spot.

A compass can do all this and more if you apply some ingenuity. And when used with a map, it can do even more. A compass makes orienting the map easier and more accurate. In addition, you can pinpoint your position, identify landmarks, and find courses to far-off destinations. Chapter 4 covers the essentials of using a map and compass together. For now, we'll explore what can be done with a compass alone. And that's plenty.

The Earth's Magnetic Field

The Chinese are believed to have invented a navigation compass around 2 AD, and Norse explorers used something similar to reach Iceland in the ninth century. Arab sailors and desert traders began using needles suspended from yarn by the twelfth century. But it wasn't until the 1300s that an instrument we would recognize as a modern compass was developed and commonly used.

Today's compass, even in its simplest form, is a remarkably refined instrument compared with what was in use back then (or even only 80 years ago). Yet it is still basically the same because it is controlled by something that hasn't changed much—the earth's magnetic field.

Remember in fifth-grade science class how iron filings lined up on a sheet of paper when a bar magnet was placed under it? The filings delineated the magnet's field of force. Well, the earth has the same sort of field around it, although it's not as orderly and well organized as the filings, and this complex field influences all magnetic materials,

including the tiny bar magnet that is the compass's needle.

Anything magnetic, or affected by magnetism, will try to line itself up with these forces. A compass's needle does not point to some magnetic "mother lode" at each pole, but aligns itself with the local magnetic forces flowing around it. That's an important point to remember.

As you'll notice in the drawing, lines of magnetic force run horizontal to the earth's surface near the equator but are nearly perpendicular close to the poles. Thus, the downward component of the magnetic field—which is called *dip*, or magnetic inclination—varies with location. Only along the *magnetic equator (ME)* will a compass needle lie horizontal. The farther it is from this zone, the more the north end (or south, in the southern hemisphere) of the needle dips downward.

In extreme cases, the needle will dip enough to keep it from swinging properly. To compensate for this, manufacturers counterbalance needles for specific magnetic zones. Compasses sold for use in the U.S. should be compensated for the zone called "magnetic north" (MN). If you are navigating in a different zone, you will need to buy a compass specifically compensated for the region.

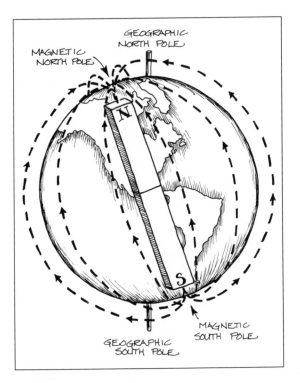

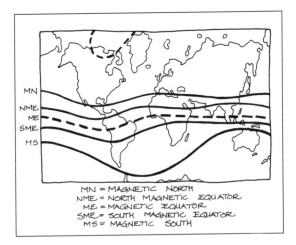

MN = MAGNETIC NORTH
NME = NORTH MAGNETIC EQUATOR
ME = MAGNETIC EQUATOR
SME = SOUTH MAGNETIC EQUATOR
MS = MAGNETIC SOUTH

How Compasses Work

The workings of a compass could hardly be simpler. The needle pivots in response to the earth's magnetic field and stops when it's aligned with the forces. The needle's north end then points to an encircling ring marked in degrees, thereby enabling us to determine directions.

As we'll see when we investigate the different compass types, there are many variations on this theme. But the above explanation describes pretty much how most compasses do their job.

While the workings of a compass are straightforward, there are some fine points to be aware of. One of the first things you might ask when choosing a compass is, "How good and accurate an instrument will I need?" The answer is, "One that will give you directions within two to four degrees. One that is rugged enough to take abuse, compact enough to fit in a pocket, and simple enough to use easily."

Some surveyor's compasses are accurate to within a few minutes (there are 60 minutes in one degree), but this is too precise for our needs. Besides, their weight, complexity, delicacy, and cost make them impractical. Since the kind of compass work we'll be doing involves large, easy-to-locate objects (roads, trails, hills, streams, lakes) rather than pinpoints in the wilderness, four degrees of accuracy is sufficient.

One degree of error will put you only about 100 feet off your mark after a one-mile walk. A four-degree error will put you off by 400 feet. In any case, the average person can't maintain a compass course to within any less than two degrees, and has to work hard to do that.

Spending more money for a compass will not necessarily get you greater accuracy. Anything over $20 (U.S. dollars in 1995) is paying for extra options and gadgets, not precision. The desired accuracy can be found in all but the cheapest models (which might still give you a workable four degrees). Most of the compasses offered by the manufacturers listed in the Appendix will do the job.

To be accurate, the needle must be well damped so it doesn't swing wildly about. Most

Certainly my own most memorable hikes can be classified as Shortcuts that Backfired.

—The Journey Home
Edward Abbey
Dutton, 1977

compasses damp excessive motion by sealing the needle in a case filled with alcohol or light petroleum oil. Test yours by quickly rotating the whole compass 90 degrees. The needle should move no more than 10 degrees, and return to north within three to five seconds. If it swings along with the compass or oscillates back and forth before settling on north, it is poorly damped—making it unreliable and hard to work with in the field.

A small bubble may appear in the liquid at extremely low temperatures (below–40°F or so) or at high altitudes (above 20,000 feet). This will not degrade performance as long as it goes away when conditions return to normal. Do not buy a compass that already has a bubble. The seal may be broken. And do not buy a compass that is pointing in a different direction from all the others in the display case. Individuality in a compass is not a positive trait!

As important as accuracy is rugged construction, for no matter how much you try to protect it, your compass will lead a hard life. To make its life easier (and longer) choose one that is compact enough to fit in a shirt or outer pack pocket. You'll also want a compass that is easy to use. Human nature being what it is, what is simple to use gets used the most. The more you refer to your compass and put it to use, the better your chances of not getting lost.

Make Your Own

Be careful with your compass. Hang it by a lanyard around your neck and tuck it under your shirt, or in a button-down pocket. If there's room, stow a small backup compass in your pack, or carry a cheap one that hangs from a zipper pull, pins to your shirt, or attaches to a watchband. Everyone in the group should have his or her own.

But things happen. You step on your compass, drop it off a cliff, or lose it over the side of the canoe. No need to worry. All is not lost. You can always make your own.

Take any piece of iron or steel that is long, thin, and light. Aluminum or yellow metals won't work. Only things that rust will do. A pin or needle is perfect, but a straightened paperclip, piece of steel baling wire or barbed wire, or the clip from a pen (careful, some are chrome or aluminum) could also work.

Now, you want that piece of metal to rotate easily. If you are sure that absolutely no drafts will influence it, you can suspend it from a thread. You will get more reliable results, though, if you float the metal on still water using balled-up paper, a wood chip, or a leaf. Gather some water in a *nonmagnetic* container or a scooped-out recess in the ground, such as a puddle. Resist the temptation to use a "tin" can, which is made of steel. (An aluminum can would be fine). Place the float on the water, then the metal on it. It will slowly turn to orient itself.

For faster, more positive results, magnetize the metal by rubbing it in one direction with a magnet. Using one end of the magnet only, rub it the length of your compass "needle," lifting the magnet up into the air a few inches after you've reached the end, and returning to the beginning of the needle before descending for another stroke in the same direction. Keep up this steady circle for six to a dozen strokes, and your needle should be well magnetized.

The magnets you are most likely to have with you are those in the speaker or headphones of a radio. Soft steel tends to lose its magnetism fairly quickly, so you might have to remagnetize your needle occasionally, though you shouldn't have to do this more than two or three times in a day.

What if you don't have a magnet? You can improve the direction-finding ability of your pointer by rubbing it (as you would with a magnet) with a stone, a piece of silk, or a piece of synthetic material. You could also magnetize it with electric currents if you should happen to have a battery and insulated wire.

Test your compass by disturbing it after it settles. Do this several times. If it returns to the same alignment, you're OK. It will be lined up north and south, though you will have to infer by other means which end is north. Use the sun, stars, or any other natural signs in the area. (See Chapter 6.)

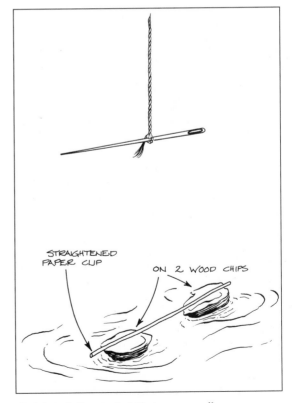

Quick-and-dirty makeshift compass needles.

Declination

In Chapter 2 we learned of two norths. The first is geographic north, also known as true north, at one end of the axis around which the earth spins. Mapmakers, by convention, place geographic north at the "top" of the world.

The second is magnetic north, at the northern end of the planet's magnetic core, west of Baffin Island.

Maps and charts use geographic north, but the compass is attracted to magnetic north. On land maps the difference between the two is called *declination*, and it varies with your position on the globe.

You need to know the local declination when you want to convert the compass's magnetic readings to a map's geographic directions, or vice versa. But of course, that need arises only when you use both a map and a compass. When you navigate by compass or map alone, you can ignore declination completely.

Nevertheless, the most accurate and dependable way to navigate is to use both, which means that

sooner or later you'll need to deal with declination.

Declination is measured in degrees and designated either east (E) or west (W). For example, in New York City the declination was about 14 degrees west (14° W) in 1994, pulling a compass's magnetized needle to the west of true north by 14 degrees to point at 346 degrees on a properly oriented geographic scale.

In San Diego the declination was about 14 degrees east (14° E) in 1994, pulling a compass needle 14 degrees east of true north to read 014 degrees on the geographic scale.

There are places where declination is greater, places where it is less, and places (such as parts of Michigan, Indiana, Ohio, Kentucky, Tennessee, and North and South Carolina) where it doesn't exist at all. You can see where by looking at an *isogonic chart*. (Isogonic means "equal angle.")

The lines on an isogonic chart connect points of equal angles of declination, just as contour lines connect points of equal altitude. As you can see, the pattern of magnetic forces is not particularly orderly—not at all like the neatly regimented iron filings in the fifth-grade bar-magnet experiment. Note the agonic ("no-angle") lines where there is no declination at all. At these spots magnetic north coincides with geographic north.

The earth's magnetic field is not only irregular, it also moves, creeping slowly westward. For example, the agonic (0 declination) line that is now west of Florida went through the center of that peninsula in 1970. This movement is called the *annual westward change.*

But don't let all this daunt you. It's not as chaotic as it might seem. To find your local declination, all you have to do is look at the declination diagram on your topographical map. There, too, you will usually find the annual westward change—which in most places is an increase or decrease of only a few minutes per year. To see if you will have to make corrections for the annual change, look in the legend to find the year the map was compiled. If it was some years ago, you might have to calculate the change in declination since then.

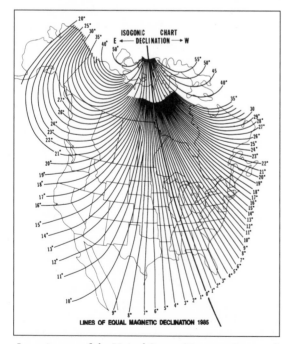

Isogonic map of the United States. (Courtesy Brunton)

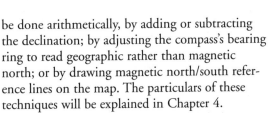

Don't ever be misled into believing you can ignore declination. It's sometimes natural to wish the compass needle were pointing to true north, but wishing won't make it so. There are parts of Alaska where declination is so great, more than 24° E on the west end of the North Slope, that if you didn't adjust for it you'd find yourself more than a third of a mile off course after a one-mile walk. Even just a few degrees of declination, when combined with compass inaccuracies and reading errors, can get you into trouble. And if you are making a long trip, check each new map's declination as you go. It will change slightly, especially if your route runs east or west.

When using a compass with a map, you must compensate for the effect of declination. This can be done arithmetically, by adding or subtracting the declination; by adjusting the compass's bearing ring to read geographic rather than magnetic north; or by drawing magnetic north/south reference lines on the map. The particulars of these techniques will be explained in Chapter 4.

If you don't know the current local declination and your map or trail guide isn't telling you, you can measure it. Take a compass bearing from one mapped object to another, and compare your reading with the bearing on the map. The difference between the two is local declination, provided you weren't holding your compass near a metal canteen when you took the bearing!

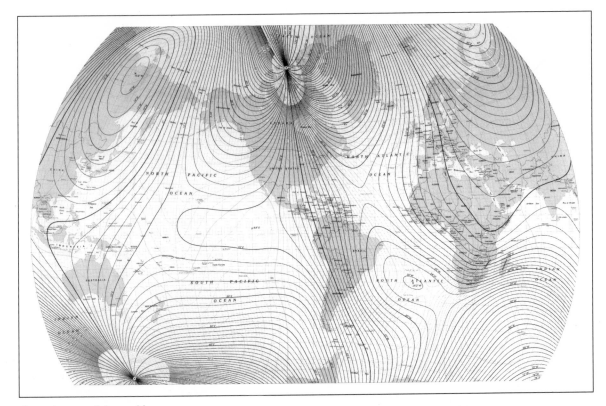

Isogonic map of the world.

Compass Types

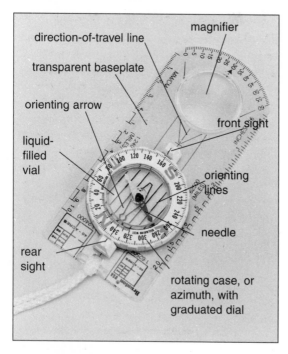

direction-of-travel line
magnifier
transparent baseplate
orienting arrow
front sight
liquid-filled vial
orienting lines
needle
rear sight
rotating case, or azimuth, with graduated dial

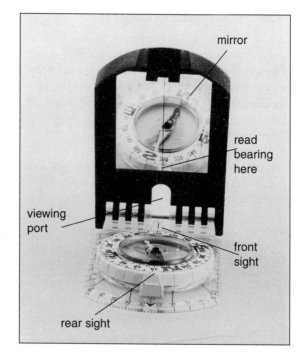

mirror
read bearing here
viewing port
front sight
rear sight

The Baseplate Compass

These are often called orienteering compasses because they were invented in 1928 by Gunnar Tillander, an unemployed instrument maker in Sweden, for the sport of orienteering, in which contestants use a map and compass to seek out a series of landmarks as quickly as possible. They've made navigating so much easier that they've since been adopted as the standard for wilderness travel, and are now the most common type available from outdoor suppliers.

They are nothing more than a simple fixed-dial compass (see below) mounted so that it rotates on a transparent baseplate. The rotating case is marked in two- or five-degree increments running clockwise around its dial. The clear center portion of the case has north/south orienting lines as well as an orienting arrow that makes it easy to align the needle with the "N" mark (north).

What makes the baseplate compass so practical is that it gives you a choice of indicating directions either with or without the use of numbered

degrees. The base doubles as a protractor for determining bearings from a map, and its edges are inscribed with map scales or a ruler to measure map distances. Almost all include an adjustment you can use to compensate for declination, converting magnetic bearings to geographic ones that can be used directly with a map.

Other nice but unnecessary additions are a magnifier to help read small map details, a clinometer to see how steep a slope is, or a sighting mirror. This last item is a flip-up mirror with a vertical line inscribed down its center. You raise the mirror, hold the compass so the line on the mirror crosses the needle's pivot point, look across the notched sight, and read the dial's reflection where the mirror's line crosses it.

Baseplate compasses are simple to use, easy to refer to in the field, extremely versatile, and relatively inexpensive—which is why they should be your first choice when purchasing a compass. For these reasons, much of the information presented later in this book presumes the use of a baseplate compass.

The Fixed-Dial Compass

These are the simplest compasses. A needle is free to pivot on a bearing and rotate within a case marked in degrees running clockwise around its circumference. They are good basic tools, and because there is not much to them they tend to be cheaper than other types. They are not used for serious navigation, however.

Fixed-dial compasses are hard to read with accuracy, so it is not wise to spend a lot of money on one. Admittedly, people found their way through the great unknown for centuries with this type of compass. But then there was no alternative, and there were no statistics on the number of navigators who got lost. Today, other compasses are more versatile and easier to use. If you already have a fixed-dial compass, by all means use it. Better yet, take it along in your pack as a backup for the more practical baseplate compass.

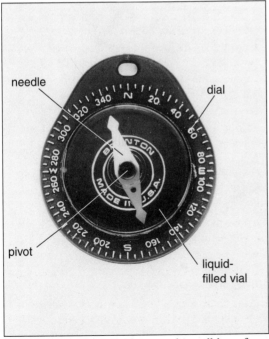

An inexpensive fixed-dial compass that will hang from a zipper pull.

The Magnetic-Card Compass

The classic compass, as seen in the previous two examples, has a needle free to rotate on its pivot around a fixed dial. But in the magnetic-card compass, needle and dial are joined (on a card) to rotate as one unit. The advantage is that "N" (north) on the card is always aligned with magnetic north, so there are no extra steps needed to orient the compass before taking a reading. The disadvantage is that you can't compensate for declination. Conversions from magnetic readings to geographic, or back, must be done by arithmetic. You'll find instructions in the Appendix.

If all your route-finding will be done with compass alone, and no maps, the magnetic-card type will work quite well. The most common examples of this type are the military-style compass with a small lens to magnify the reading, and compasses sold for use in boats or automobiles.

The military compass has a forward and a rear sight for aiming the instrument. You look through the sights at a landmark, then through the lens to read the bearing indicated by the lubber line, a mark on the forward part of the case in line with the sights. It is thought to have got its unusual name in the early days of sailing ships, when sailors thought only a lubber (clumsy oaf) needed this forward-pointing line to guide a vessel. The purpose of the sights and the lens is to improve bearing accuracy. Compared with baseplate compasses, this type is not as versatile, can't be easily used with a map, and is only theoretically more accurate, which is why outdoor equipment suppliers rarely stock them. They can usually be found in military surplus outlets. If you already have one, by all means learn its ways and use it.

Marine/automobile magnetic-card compasses are ideal for use in almost any vehicle: boats, snowmobiles, trucks, even dog sleds. No matter what direction the vehicle is pointing, the lubber line will show that bearing. All you have to do is mount the compass so you can view the lubber line directly, and so that the central pivot of the compass and the lubber line are parallel to the vehicle's centerline. This ensures that both compass and vehicle point in the same direction.

Any compass mounted near ferrous metals or electrical currents will be erratic. In a car, or wherever these potentially disturbing influences are found, the compass will deviate from its alignment with the earth's magnetic field. In all but the cheapest boat or car compass, this deviation can compensated for, partially if not completely, with adjustable internal magnets.

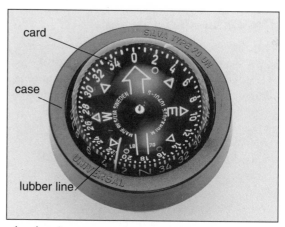

Auto/marine compass.

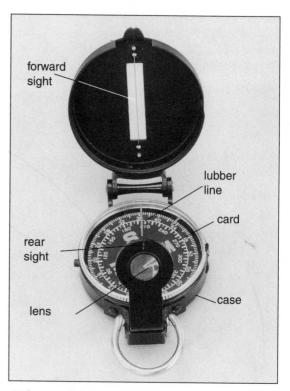

Military-style lensatic compass.

What is it that makes it so hard sometimes to determine whither we will walk? I believe that there is a subtle magnetism in Nature, which, if we unconsciously yield to it, will direct us aright.

—*from "Walking"*
Henry David Thoreau

Orienting Your Compass to Magnetic North

1: The baseplate compass.

With the orienting arrow pointing to "N" (north) on the case's dial, hold the baseplate and then rotate the case so the needle is enclosed within the orienting arrow's outline. The compass is now ori-

ented to magnetic north and directions can be read from where the direction-of-travel line intersects the case's dial.

2: The fixed-dial compass.

The premise of this compass's operation is that the needle always stays aligned with magnetic north. The north end of the needle will be painted red, striped, marked with an "N," or shaped like an arrowhead. Once the needle has settled in position, turn the whole compass so the printed "N" (north, or 360 degrees) on the dial comes under the north end of the needle. The compass is now oriented to magnetic north and directions can be read from it.

3: The magnetic-card compass.

This compass is always aligned with magnetic north and no extra steps are needed before taking a bearing.

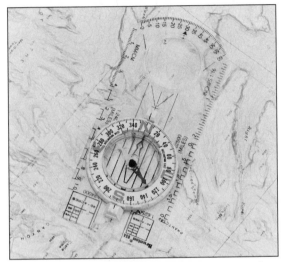

Baseplate compass needle and orienting arrow out of alignment.

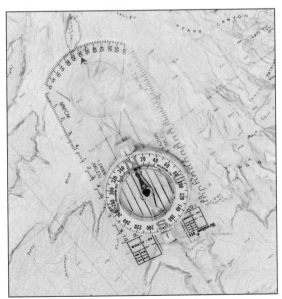

Needle aligned with orienting arrow. The compass sits on a Trails Illustrated *map of Zion National Park.*

A fixed-dial compass oriented to magnetic north. The bearing of any visible object can now be read from the dial. The Canadian topo covers a piece of Ontario east of Georgian Bay.

Orienting Your Compass to Geographic North

1: *The baseplate compass.*

One of the nicest features of baseplate compasses is that almost all of them can be adjusted to compensate for declination. The method is different for each manufacturer but the principle is the same. The clear center portion of the case, with the north/south orienting lines and arrow, can be rotated within the case's outer dial.

When you purchase the compass, the orienting arrow will be pointing to "N," so the compass will read magnetic directions. But if you rotate the center of the case so the orienting arrow is offset from "N" by the amount of your local declination, the compass will read in geographic directions.

All you are doing is moving the magnetic north indicator to coincide with its true bearing. Now, when you read the compass it will be in directions that relate to those on a map, with no need to bother further about declination.

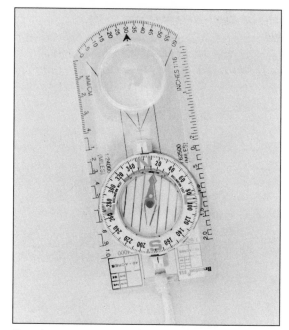

Baseplate compass oriented to geographic north in a place (such as San Diego in 1994) where the declination is 14 degrees east . . .

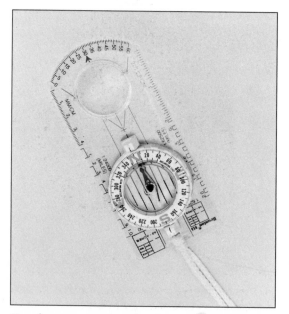

Baseplate compass oriented to magnetic north. All readings will be in degrees magnetic.

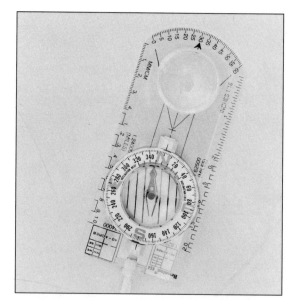

. . . and in a place (such as New York City in 1994) where it is 14 degrees west. In both cases all readings will be in "true" or "map" degrees.

2: The fixed-dial compass.

When using this compass with a map you have to correct for declination. One way is by addition or subtraction. It's simple enough, but if you tend to become confused, especially at times of stress, you don't need to bother with it. It is explained in the Appendix for those who are interested.

An easier way to compensate for declination is by putting a mark or piece of tape on the case. When the needle points to the mark, the compass is oriented to geographic north. For example, with 14 degrees west declination, put the mark 14 degrees west of the dial's north (at 346 degrees). With 14 degrees east declination, put the mark 14 degrees east of the dial's north (at 014 degrees).

3: The magnetic-card compass.

With this compass, there's no way physically to compensate for declination. To convert its magnetic readings to true or geographic bearings, you have no option but to use simple arithmetic.

Above: Fixed-dial compass oriented to geographic north where the local declination is 14 degrees east . . .
Below: . . . and where it is 14 degrees west. All readings will be in "true" or "map" degrees.

Bearings

A bearing is the direction of one object from another, measured as a horizontal angle from a fixed baseline. In our case, that baseline is either true north or magnetic north. When taking a bearing with a baseplate compass or a fixed-dial compass, always hold it straight in front of you. Looking at it from the side will not give you a correct reading.

On compasses with an optional direction-of-travel arrow, this manually set pointer is used as a memory aid to mark the desired bearing on the dial.

All compass work is based on three types of bearings:

Direct Bearings

Whether you know your position or not, a compass will tell you the direction toward a landmark you can identify on the map. For example: "The compass shows that the tower bears 060 degrees from my position." (Incidentally, careful navigators always use the three-digit notation with bearings, to avoid confusion.)

Here's how you can measure that bearing with your compass:

1: The baseplate compass.

Hold the compass level at your waist or chest, and in your left hand (if you're right-handed). Point the direction-of-travel line at the landmark. Turn the case with your right hand until the orienting arrow is aligned with the north end of needle. Read the bearing where the direction-of-travel line intersects the case's dial.

2: The fixed-dial compass.

Face the landmark. Hold the compass level in both hands at your waist or chest, making "pointers" with the two index fingers. Aim at the landmark. Orient the compass by rotating it between your fingers until the needle points to "N". Read the direct bearing in degrees on the far side of the dial along an imaginary line connecting the pivot and the landmark.

3: The magnetic-card compass.

Look straight at the lubber line. Sighting at an angle will give you an incorrect reading.

Extend an imaginary line from the central pivot through the lubber line to the landmark. The bearing is read where the lubber line intersects the card.

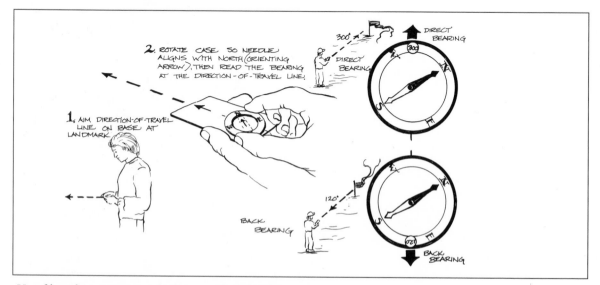

Use of baseplate compass to take direct and back bearings.

Reciprocal or "Back" Bearings

When you don't know your exact position, a compass will tell you the direction from a landmark to where you stand (which is the reciprocal, or dead opposite, of the direct bearing). For example: "My position bears 240 degrees from that tower."

Here's how to do it with your compass:

1: The baseplate compass.

Hold the compass level at your waist or chest, and in your left hand (if you're right-handed). Point the direction-of-travel line at the landmark. Turn the case with your right hand until the orienting arrow is aligned with the south end of the needle. Read the back bearing where the direction-of-travel line intersects the case's dial.

Because a back bearing is the exact opposite of a direct bearing, it differs from it by 180 degrees, so it's simple to calculate one from the other. If the direct bearing you observe is 180 degrees or greater, subtract 180 degrees to get the back bearing. If the direct bearing is less than 180 degrees, add 180 degrees to the direct bearing to get the back bearing.

2: The fixed-dial compass.

Follow the steps for taking a direct bearing. Read the back bearing in degrees on the near side of the dial along the extension of an imaginary line connecting the pivot and the landmark. Or, after the direct bearing has been taken,

rotate the compass so the north end of the needle points to the degree notation of the direct bearing instead of to north ("N"). The south end of the needle will indicate the back bearing.

Once again, you can easily calculate a back bearing. If the direct bearing is greater then 180 degrees, subtract 180 degrees to get the back bearing. If the direct bearing is less than 180 degrees, add 180 to get the back bearing.

3: The magnetic-card compass.

Take a direct bearing as explained previously. If the direct bearing is greater than 180 degrees, subtract 180 degrees to get the back bearing. If the direct bearing is less than 180 degrees, add 180 degrees to get the back bearing.

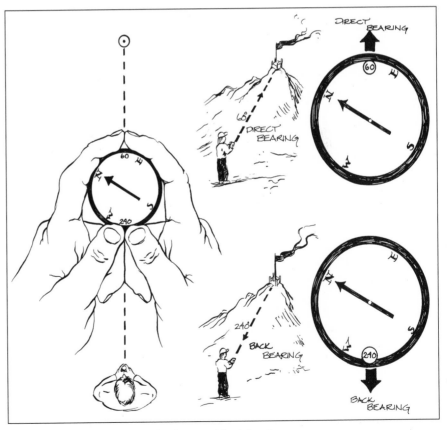

Use of fixed-dial compass to take direct and back bearings.

Finding a Landmark

You can locate a landmark by sighting along a known bearing. For example: "I should be able to find the tower on a bearing of 060 degrees." Here's how to do it with your compass:

1: The baseplate compass.

Turn the case's dial so the bearing to be set coincides with the direction-of-travel line. Hold the compass level with both hands at your waist or chest. Turn your whole body until the orienting arrow is aligned with the north end of the needle. Look along the direction-of-travel line to find the landmark.

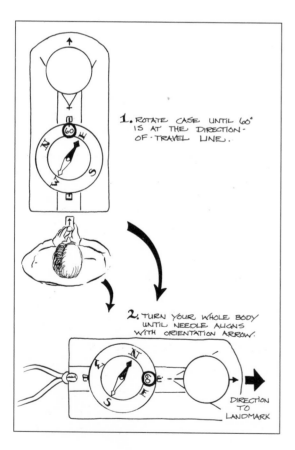

2: The fixed-dial compass.

Hold the compass level in both hands at your waist or chest, making "pointers" with the two index fingers. The pointers should be an extension of an imaginary line connecting the pivot and the known bearing on the dial. Turn your whole body until the compass is oriented with the needle pointing to "N." Look in the direction of the pointers to find the landmark.

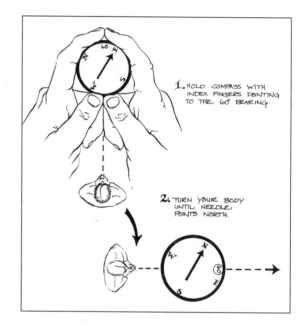

3: The magnetic-card compass.

Point the compass so the desired bearing lies on the lubber line. Sight along an imaginary line from the central pivot through the lubber line to find the landmark.

Deviation

The earth's magnetic field is not a particularly powerful force. You won't find it lining up your refrigerator magnets every morning. So the magnetic needle, or card, of a compass has to be very sensitive. Sensitive enough that it can be unintentionally deflected from its natural alignment by everyday objects. Keep your compass away from radios, knives, belt buckles (even ones that look like brass), cameras, battery-powered watches, guns, overhead power lines, and railroad tracks. And never put it on the hood of your car to do map work!

Any irregular influence that overrides the natural magnetic field is called *deviation*. It's a good idea to check for deviation before heading out. Do this with your full pack on and holding the compass as you would on the trail. When using a map, take bearings from a known position to identifiable landmarks. When at an unknown position, use transits, as described earlier. Correct for declination, and see if the compass's readings match those from the map. If you have no map, check your bearings against someone else's compass. Or use the north star, or the sun (see Chapter 6). If your bearings seem weird, look for deviation.

Areas of serious magnetic disturbance are usually marked on maps and nautical charts. On land, there are many places where magnetic anomalies occur, in mountainous or hilly terrain and in other areas, because of ore deposits.

In northern latitudes, watch out for "bog iron" in, or near to, large, flat heath-bog terrain. These deposits may throw a compass off many degrees.

Beware, too, of deviation you introduce yourself—apart from the belt buckles and radios already mentioned. Think what's fairly near your compass when you take a sight—in your backpack, maybe. Metal flashlights and batteries are notorious for affecting compasses. Beware of the ferrous metal in your eyeglass frames when you hold a compass to your eye. And if you have a pacemaker, well, you might just have to ask someone else to take the sight for you.

Compensating for Deviation

There is no need to compensate a hand-held compass. If it doesn't seem right, step a few feet to one side, or put it down so you are not holding it. The deviation should disappear.

Although I prefer to navigate with just a map, I always carry a compass. For trail travel, it's hardly ever needed, except perhaps when you arrive at an unsigned junction in thick mist or dense forest, and aren't sure which branch to follow. Once you strike out cross-country, though, a compass may prove essential.

—The Backpacker's Handbook
Chris Townsend
Ragged Mountain Press, 1993

Following a Compass Course

Part 1: Going Straight

A compass will help you maintain a straight course toward an objective, even if you lose sight of your objective along the way. You'll need its help because you can't walk a straight course on your own. As we discussed in Chapter 1, people tend to veer off in a circle (usually clockwise) when they are cut off from sensory reference. This can happen in snow, fog, rain, night, or in a thick forest. Even if you think you'll be able to see your destination at all times, use a compass anyway—be prepared.

A good example of where this might be necessary is when passing through thick woods to reach a destination that will be obscured from view most of the way. It would seem that all you have to do is take a bearing of your destination at the start and then follow that heading on the compass. But it's not that easy.

First, take the bearing toward your objective. Write it down so you won't forget it or, when using a baseplate compass, be careful not to rotate the case and accidentally move the orienting arrow. Once you have the bearing, don't just set off in that direction. Look ahead to the limit of your vision and pick a distinctive intermediate landmark on that same bearing. Then put the compass away and walk to the landmark. But before you go, find or make a recognizable landmark at the spot you are leaving, so that you can check your course by referring back to your starting place.

If you try to watch the compass while you're walking, you'll wind up stepping off a cliff or sustaining world-class shin damage from tripping over logs. Just walk to your chosen intermediate landmark by the easiest route. It doesn't have to be straight. Once there, take out the compass and sight along your original bearing to find the next intermediate landmark, and walk to that. Proceed in small steps, checking yourself along the way while heading on your original bearing. Repeat until you've reached your destination.

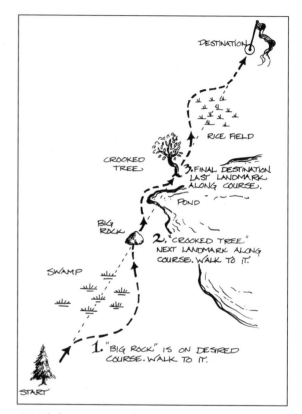

Divide long trips into short segments. Pick landmarks that will not be obscured, and try to keep your intermediate goal and starting point in view as you walk.

Part 2: Lateral Drift

The reason for making a series of short jumps instead of one long compass run is lateral drift. A compass bearing without a visible destination gives you only forward direction. Using only a bearing, you have no way of knowing if you have strayed to one side or the other of it. This is why it is so important to maintain visual contact with both your starting point and an intermediate landmark.

But what happens when you lose sight of your intermediate landmark? To check if you are still headed toward it, take a back bearing from where you are to the spot you just left. This is why it is important to mark or remember your last position. If the back bearing is not 180 degrees from your original bearing, walk to one side or the other until it is. Then turn around and sight ahead along the original bearing. Your intermediate landmark should be off in that direction.

Don't just keep plowing ahead on your original bearing after losing the landmark. Lateral drift may have occurred. The compass will assure you that you are on the correct bearing. But there are an infinite number of similar bearings all lying parallel to each other, with only one connecting your starting point and the landmark. The only way to find that one is by taking a back bearing.

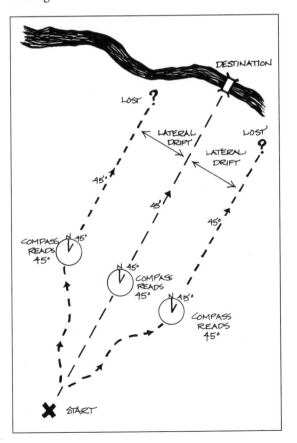

Part 3: With No Landmarks

Though it is not likely, there may come a time in flat, open country when no intermediate landmarks can be found. You can see your destination far off in the haze, but if night, the weather, or anything else blocks it from view you could be in trouble. When nature doesn't provide landmarks, ingenuity is needed.

One way to be sure you'll proceed in a straight line is to make your own transit. When two widely spaced objects appear to line up, you know you are on an extension of the line (the transit) that connects them. But please do not erect transit markers that you will leave behind—such as a cairn (pile of rocks) or a branch stuck in the ground with a scrap of cloth on it. The proliferation of "bad cairns" is a problem in many parks and wilderness areas. They are often the reason inexperienced parties get lost, since they were built by people who were themselves "lost." And a marker that involves litter is doubly harmful.

If you're with a group, send someone ahead to the limit of your vision on the desired bearing. Use hand signals, and your compass set with the bearing, to position the person as a human intermediate landmark. Your human marker then double-checks with a back bearing. When all is set, your marker stays put, you join him or her, and then start the process over again.

It's also possible to hold a reasonably straight course for a short distance, even if you have no compass and can't see any landmarks. By having at least three people walking in single file and spaced far apart, the last member of the group will be able to tell if the lead is veering off course. Don't count on it for too long, though. If the last person goes off course, or even the middle one, the whole group will go astray.

There may not be a single wilderness in the lower 48 states, and no more than a very few in Alaska and Canada, that is featureless enough to require artificial transits. If you're traveling solo over a featureless landscape, you may wish to take

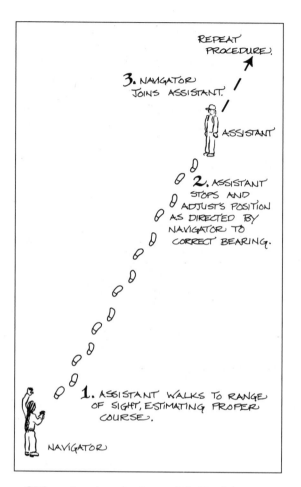

REPEAT
PROCEDURE.

3. NAVIGATOR
JOINS ASSISTANT.

ASSISTANT

2. ASSISTANT
STOPS AND
ADJUSTS POSITION
AS DIRECTED BY
NAVIGATOR TO
CORRECT BEARING.

1. ASSISTANT WALKS TO RANGE
OF SIGHT, ESTIMATING PROPER
COURSE.

NAVIGATOR

a GPS receiver (see the Appendix). Don't leave a trail of blazes, cairns, or other markings behind you.

Part 4: Around Obstacles

Sometimes you head off on a straight course and encounter an unforeseen obstacle. Whether it's a precipice, rough ground, a bog, or a field of nasty-looking bulls, you'll have to find your way around it without being thrown off course. There are two variations on this situation.

In one, you can see where you want to go but can't walk directly to it. A river blocks your way and the only place to ford it is far upstream. Or maybe your course would take you through a

poison-ivy patch. The solution is to use an intermediate landmark.

Find a marker where you stop, look to the other side of the obstacle for an intermediate landmark that is on your course, and then get to it any way you can. Confirm that you have reached the landmark, and that it is on your course, with a back bearing to your starting point. When there is no obvious landmark on the opposite side, you will either have to send someone around to act as a human landmark, or, if you're alone, go around and take back bearings on the starting point until you regain your course.

In the other variation, you can't see across or through whatever is in your way. This could be a hill, a dense swamp, or fog on a lake. The only way to pick up your bearing on the other side is to make a detour with a series of short, right-angle legs. Here's how.

Turn 90 degrees from your course and walk until you are clear of the obstruction, counting your steps as you go. Then turn 90 degrees back onto the original course and continue walking (no

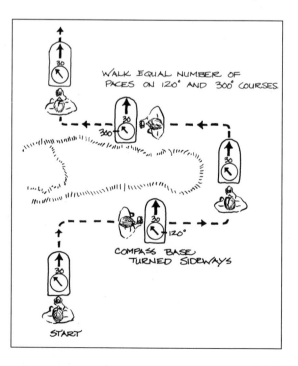

WALK EQUAL NUMBER OF
PACES ON 120° AND 300° COURSES.

COMPASS BASE
TURNED SIDEWAYS

START

need to count steps this time). Turn 90 degrees once more, this time walking back toward your base course line, counting out the same number of steps as you did on the first leg. The lengths of the two "out" and "back" legs must be equal, which is why keeping track of the number of steps you take is important.

This technique can be done with any compass by adding or subtracting the 90 degrees. It will be a lot easier, though, if you use a baseplate compass. Without moving the orienting arrow, and keeping the needle in place, you sight along the back edge on the leg out and the leg back. This automatically gives you 90-degree turns, with no chance of losing or forgetting your original course.

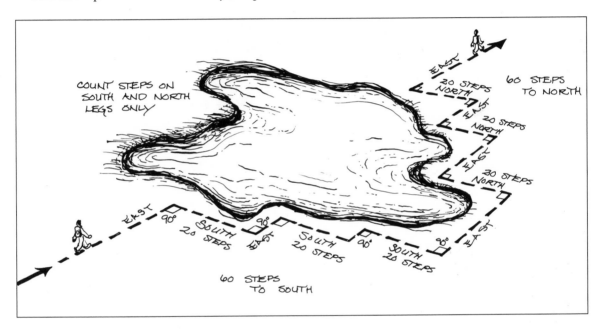

Testing Your Skills

The difference between thinking we can do something by just reading about it, and actually doing it is always greater than we expect. As easy as compass work is, and it is easy, it still won't be anything like what you thought it would be when the time comes to turn knowledge into action.

Now is the time, before it becomes a matter either of getting home or spending the night lost, to come to terms with your compass. Learn how you interact with it and read it. See what its idiosyncrasies are, and yours. Pick up your compass and this book, find an open field, and do these exercises:

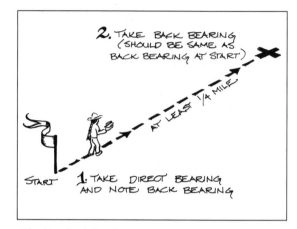

Checking back bearings.

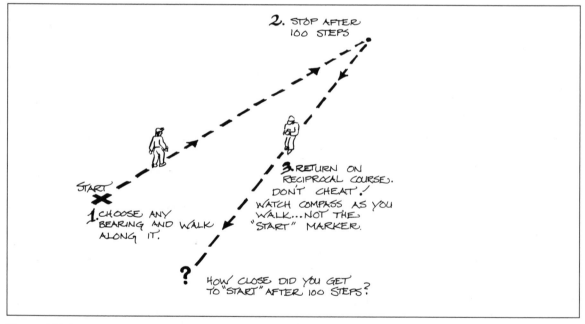

Out-and-back accuracy.

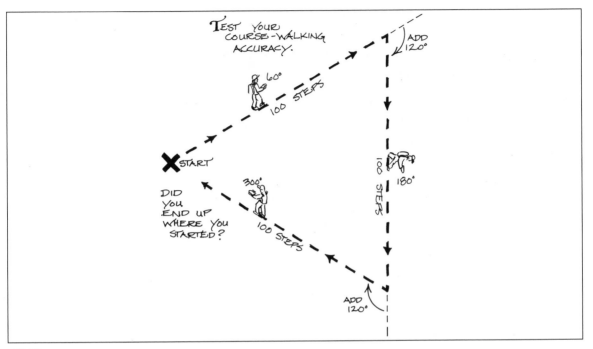

Walking a course.

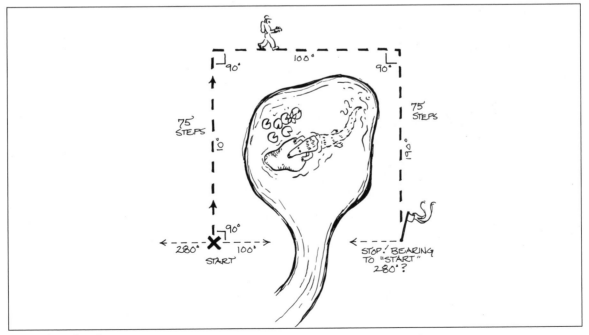

Around an obstacle.

Chapter Four

NAVIGATION

Having become familiar with maps and compasses, we are ready to combine them, merging the two into something called navigation. It's a big jump, and a definite improvement over being just a map reader or compass user. The principles of navigation are easy to acquire and simple to apply, and once grasped they make getting lost more difficult than staying found. Navigation is about motion. It's the ability to travel without getting disoriented. While surveying or position-finding gives you your immediate location, navigation not only tells you where you are, but where you've been, where you will be, how to get there, when you'll get there, and how to get back. It's based on a common universal reference—north. No matter where you go, north stays put. With a compass and map aligned toward north, you have an almost foolproof way of staying oriented. And that is what this chapter is about, the use of map and compass to keep track of your ever-changing position as you travel through the wilderness.

Of course, there is the problem of having two norths—one geographic, the other magnetic. You'll have to choose one to base your navigation on. But this, too, is simple. You can use either one, choosing whichever best suits your needs.

With that in mind, and map and compass in hand, we begin a series of bearing-taking techniques, matching directions between map and compass. You'll pick out a direction on the map and convert it to a course you can follow on the compass. Bearings will also be used to locate an object whose only proof of existence is a mark on the map. Or the other way around, to find on the map what you see in front of you. Then there are special bearings, *lines of position*, that tell you where you are when you haven't a clue. Lines of position can pinpoint you on the map, let you return to that same place, and keep you out of danger. Finally there's some helpful esoterica about distance—how far you've gone and how far still to go—and how that's used to keep track of where you are.

After this chapter you'll be able to find your way out and back from almost anywhere in the world. If you were worried before, you should no longer have any fear of getting lost. This fear, which exists to some degree in all of us, can in extreme cases keep you from exploring new places and stifle the spirit of adventure which, if you've read this far, is probably a significant part of your nature. Soon you'll have what it takes to get out there and enjoy the wilderness with one less thing to worry about.

Map and Compass Combined

Choosing a Point of Reference

To navigate successfully you must choose one reference point and relate all directions to it. By convention, and for convenience, we use north as that point—either geographic or magnetic.

Maps are based on geographic north. The vertical lines of longitude that run up and down the map connect the geographic north and south poles. When you derive a direction from a map, the course is given in reference to geographic north.

Compasses, on the other hand, use magnetic north, which can vary from geographic north by as much as 21 degrees in the contiguous United States, and even more in Canada and Alaska. The difference between the two norths, as we also learned earlier, is called declination on land maps, and variation on nautical charts.

Now, let's presume you're at a trail junction in a fog-shrouded valley in Colorado. The map says that by traveling toward 270 degrees you will find a cabin two miles away. If you simply walked on a course of 270 degrees according to your compass, you'd miss the cabin by more than 2,500 feet and probably wander around with growing apprehension until the fog lifted. That's because you ignored the 13 degrees of east declination relevant to this area. That's the difference between magnetic (compass) and geographic (map) directions. And that's why maps and compasses can't "talk" to each other without some translation.

Except in the few parts of the world where there is no declination, you must pick one reference point, the map's or the compass's, and translate the other to it. In navigating you can speak either "compass" or "map," but trying to use both at once guarantees that you will soon be lost.

Your choice defines the system of navigation you will be relying on. Once the selection is made for a particular journey, stay with it, or confusion and disorientation will reign.

Each system has advantages and disadvantages, as we're about to see. But most serious navigators use geographic, or true, north because the map is the primary tool. As a result, they habitually correct their compass readings for declination.

Geographic, or True, North

If you decide to use the map's geographic north as your point of reference, as most wilderness navigators do, your compass readings need to be corrected to match it. You can either do this arithmetically, or by making the compass read as if it were pointing to geographic rather than magnetic north.

Advantages.

Adapting the compass to the map, rather than the other way around, is the easiest way to compensate for declination. It is especially easy with a baseplate (orienteering) type of compass that has a built-in declination adjustment feature. You set your local

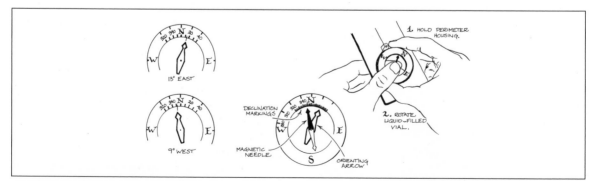

Declination adjustment in a baseplate compass. When the needle aligns with the offset orienting arrow, the compass reads to geographic north.

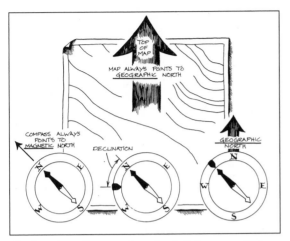

Declination adjustment in a fixed-dial compass. When the needle points to the tape, the compass reads to geographic north.

When the needle points to your new north, instead of to the inscribed "N" on the dial, all directions become relative to geographic north. See Chapter 3 for more information.

Magnetic North

If you decide to use the compass's magnetic north as your point of reference, then the directions found on a map need to be corrected to match it. You can either do this mathematically, or by drawing lines on the map that are aligned with magnetic north.

Advantages.

You can use any type of compass, with no need to buy a baseplate compass or resort to tape on a fixed-dial compass face.

Disadvantages.

It's cumbersome to convert a map to magnetic north. You have to inscribe parallel lines that are at the same angle and direction as the declination. The process requires a large flat surface, pencil, protractor, and ruler. It takes time and care. It's almost impossible to do on the trail. The procedure will have to be repeated for every map you'll need.

Making the map read magnetic north.

There are two ways. To use either, you have to know your local declination, which can be found in the map's legend, adjusted for the annual change in declination.

You can convert from geographic to magnetic by adding or subtracting the declination from what you read on the compass or find on the map. This technique is explained in the Appendix.

You can also convert the map. This requires you to draw lines aligned to magnetic north. All map directions can then be oriented to these magnetic lines, making them compatible with readings from a compass.

You could draw lines over the whole map, but that would require a lot of work and the use of a yardstick to draw such long lines.

declination and then forget about it. From then on, the compass automatically reads geographic north.

Disadvantages.

There aren't many. The declination adjustment feature on baseplate compasses adds a few dollars to the cost. The tape used on fixed-dial compasses can shift or fall off.

Making the compass read geographic north.

There are two ways. To use either you should look up your declination in the legend of a local map, correcting as necessary for the annual change in declination since your map was printed (see Chapter 3).

The first way is to use simple arithmetic. You can convert from magnetic to geographic by adding or subtracting the declination from what you read on the compass or find on the map. This technique is explained in the Appendix. While the rules are not difficult, they can be confusing, especially when you're hurried or anxious.

The faster and more reliable way is to offset your compass. You can reposition north on the compass by the same amount as the declination.

A more practical alternative is to draw lines on only the sections you will use. You can do this with a 12-inch ruler that fits in your pack. You'll also need a pencil and a plastic protractor with a 6-inch ruler (which could take the place of the 12-inch ruler if space is at a premium) on the bottom.

Here's how to proceed:

1: Connect the fine, black latitude marks on the left and right borders of the map. This will give you four horizontal lines: the two lines you just drew, and the top and bottom borders.
2: Note the declination in the map's legend.
3: Mark a point on one of the horizontal lines near where you will be traveling or taking bearings.
4: Place the protractor on the marked point and measure out the declination angle. Refer to the declination diagram to see which way MN (magnetic north) inclines. Do not use the indicators on the declination diagram to measure the angle. Use only the written degree values. The angular difference between the magnetic and geographic north indicators is only symbolic. It is not accurate.
5: Using a ruler, extend the angle as far as possible or necessary.
6: Draw lines parallel to the first, using the width of the ruler.

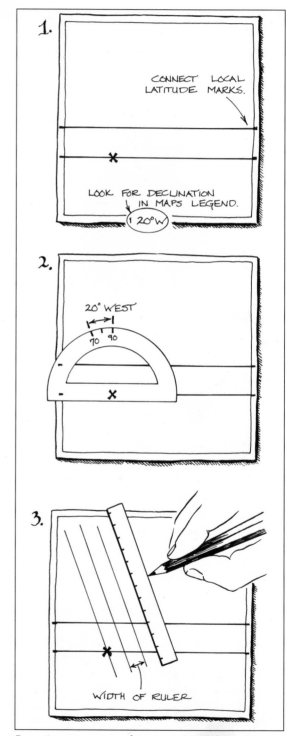

Preparing a map to read to magnetic north.

Orienting the Map with a Compass

Back in Chapter 2, we learned how to orient (align) a map to the surrounding landscape by comparing identifiable features in the field with those on the map, and then turning the map until it related to what we saw. But if you are not sure what landmarks you are looking at, or when there are no landmarks, you'll have to use a compass.

The map-and-compass exercises in this chapter will be demonstrated with a baseplate compass. It makes most procedures a lot faster and simpler.

Compass Corrected for Declination

1: The compass's declination adjustment is already offset to correspond with geographic north.
2: Rotate the compass's dial so that North (N, or 360 degrees) is at the direction-of-travel line.
3: Place the baseplate along the map's right- or left-hand border. The direction-of-travel line must be toward the top of the map.
4: Turn the map, with the compass on it, until the needle is enclosed within the orienting arrow's outline. The map is now oriented with the landscape.

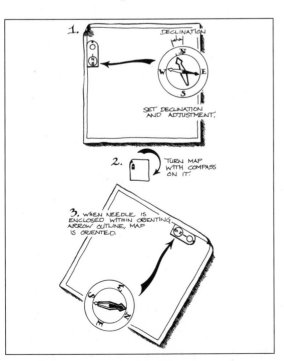

Map Corrected for Declination

1: You've already drawn lines on the map that correspond to magnetic north.
2: Rotate the compass's dial so that North (N, or 360 degrees) is at the direction-of-travel line.
3: Place the baseplate along one of the magnetic north lines drawn on the map. The direction-of-travel line must be toward the top of the map.
4: Turn the map, with the compass on it, until the needle is enclosed within the orienting arrow's outline. The map is now oriented.

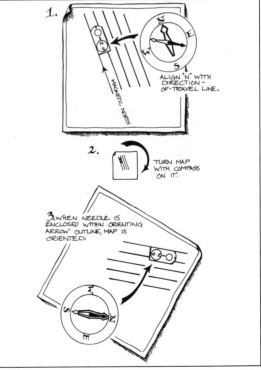

Finding a Course From the Map

This assumes that you know where you and your objective are on the map, and now need a compass course to use in the field. From the map you can determine the direction to your destination, correct for declination, and then follow your compass.

This is the job that the baseplate compass was invented for and does best. Earlier, we saw how to use a protractor to find directions on a map. Since a baseplate compass takes the place of a protractor, you now have one less piece of equipment to carry. Furthermore, once the direction is dialed into the compass, it stays locked in place to be used as a bearing in the field. The baseplate compass combines protractor, compass, and ruler in one tool.

Compass Corrected for Declination

1: Set the compass's declination adjustment.
2: Connect your position and objective with a course line that intersects one of the map's vertical borders or a line of longitude.
3: Place the compass's baseplate along the course line and its transparent case over a vertical line. The baseplate can be, and usually is, used to link position and objective.
4: Rotate the case until North and South on the dial (not the orienting arrow!) are parallel to the vertical line. For now, ignore the needle.
5: The course is shown where the direction-of-travel line intersects the dial.
6: Hold the compass in front of you and turn your whole body until the needle is enclosed within the orienting arrow's outline. Follow that course.

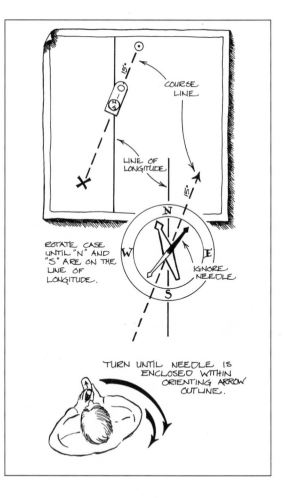

COURSE LINE

LINE OF LONGITUDE

ROTATE CASE UNTIL "N" AND "S" ARE ON THE LINE OF LONGITUDE.

IGNORE NEEDLE

TURN UNTIL NEEDLE IS ENCLOSED WITHIN ORIENTING ARROW OUTLINE.

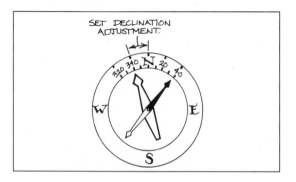

SET DECLINATION ADJUSTMENT.

Map Corrected for Declination

1: Draw lines on the map toward magnetic north.

2: Connect your position and objective with a course line that intersects one of the magnetic north lines.

3: Place the compass's baseplate along the course line and its transparent case over a magnetic north line.

4: Rotate the case until the orienting arrow is parallel to the magnetic north line. For now, ignore the needle.

5: The course is shown where the direction-of-travel line intersects the dial.

6: Hold the compass in front of you and turn your whole body until the needle is enclosed within the orienting arrow's outline. Follow that course.

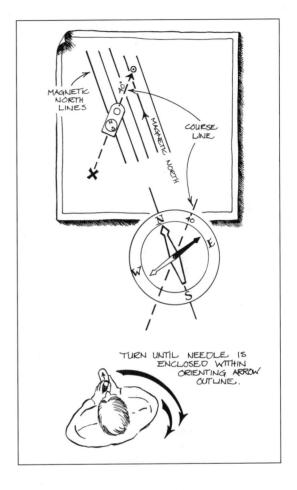

MAGNETIC NORTH LINES

COURSE LINE

MAGNETIC NORTH

TURN UNTIL NEEDLE IS ENCLOSED WITHIN ORIENTING ARROW OUTLINE.

our trio of pests still invade and obstruct us on all occasions, these are the Musquetoes eye knats and prickley pears, equal to any three curses that ever poor Egypt laiboured under.

—The Journals of Lewis and Clark
Edited by Bernard De Voto
Houghton Mifflin Company, 1953

Locating a Mapped Object in the Field

You know where you are, and you see a landmark on the map that might be helpful as a reference point. But when you look up from the map you're not sure where the landmark is. If it's a mountain peak, it could be clustered with others, making it hard to spot. What you need is the exact direction from your position to the mark.

To find that direction, draw a line on the map from your position to the known object, determine the direction from you to it, correct for declination, then aim your compass to that bearing. What it points to is the landmark you picked out on the map.

As you will have noticed, this procedure is essentially the same as the one for finding a course.

Compass Corrected for Declination

1: The compass's declination adjustment is set to correspond with geographic north.
2: Mark your position and that of the object. Connect the two with a straight line that extends until it intersects a left- or right-hand border, or a drawn-in line of longitude, which represents geographic north.
3: Place the compass's baseplate along the line toward the object. Slide the compass on this line until its pivot is over a geographic north line.
4: Rotate the case until North and South on the dial (not the orienting arrow and lines!) are parallel to the geographic north line. For now, ignore the needle.
5: The bearing to the object is shown where the direction-of-travel line intersects the dial.
6: To locate the object: Hold the compass in front of you and turn your whole body until the needle is enclosed within the orienting arrow's outline. Look along the direction-of-travel line to find the object.

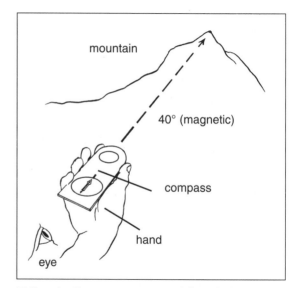

Follow the illustrations on page 94 for a declination-adjusted compass. You should see the landmark on the prescribed bearing.

Map Corrected for Declination

1: Lines are drawn on the map that correspond to magnetic north.
2: Mark your position and that of the object. Connect the two with a straight line that extends until it intersects one of the magnetic north lines.
3: Place the compass's baseplate along the line toward the object. Slide the compass on this line until its transparent case is over a magnetic north line.
4: Rotate the case until the orienting arrow is parallel to the magnetic north line. For now, ignore the needle.
5: The bearing to the object is shown where the direction-of-travel line intersects the dial.
6: To locate the object, hold the compass in front of you and turn your whole body until the needle is enclosed within the orienting arrow's outline. Look along the direction-of-travel line to find the object.

Navigation was a matter of dead reckoning, so many hours at so many miles per hour. The eye was of small assistance. Each esker looked like the last, and each clump of stunted spruce or each rock. Darkness set in shortly after noon. It was not the darkness of night, but rather of a long-extended twilight. The sun not far below the horizon and the extreme whiteness of everything lent fair visibility, but so blurred the outlines of distant knolls as to render them more alike than ever.

—Snow Man
Malcolm Waldron
Houghton Mifflin Company, 1931

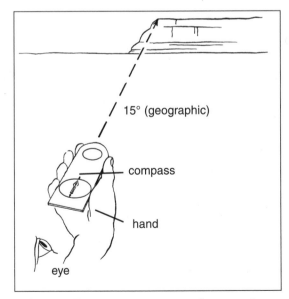

Follow the illustrations on page 93. When you sight along the bearing read from the map, you should see the landmark.

Locating an Observed Object on the Map

In previous procedures we took a direction from the map and converted it to a compass bearing. Now we'll convert a compass bearing to a direction on the map.

Let's say you see something that would make a good reference point but are not sure where, or if, it is on the map. Since you know your position, a bearing to the object will help locate it on the map. Take the bearing, correct it for declination, then transfer it to the map, drawing it outward from your position. By looking along the plotted bearing line, you should be able to identify the object.

We did a primitive version of this in Chapter 2, sighting the object along a straightedge held over an oriented map. What you will do here is far more accurate and useful. Here's how to proceed:

Compass Corrected for Declination

1: The compass's declination adjustment is set to correspond with geographic north.
2: Take a bearing by pointing the direction-of-travel line at the object and turning the case until the orienting arrow aligns with the needle. Read the bearing where the direction-of-travel line intersects the dial.
3: Mark your position. Place a side of the baseplate on your position, with the pivot over a geographic north line such as a left- or right-hand border, or a drawn-in line of longitude. The direction-of-travel line should be toward the object.
4: Turn the entire compass by the baseplate until North and South on the dial (not the orienting arrow or lines!) are parallel to the geographic north line. Ignore the needle.
5: Draw a line along the baseplate outward toward the object. You will probably have to extend this line with a ruler for it to cross an object on the map that is similar to the one you see in the field.

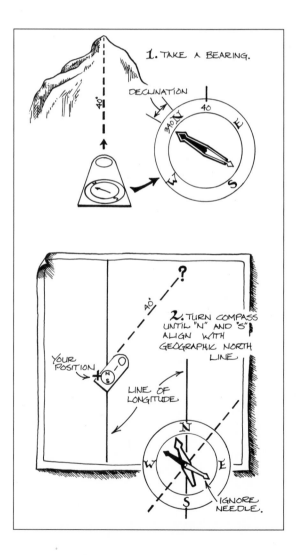

1. TAKE A BEARING.

DECLINATION

2. TURN COMPASS UNTIL "N" AND "S" ALIGN WITH GEOGRAPHIC NORTH LINE.

YOUR POSITION

LINE OF LONGITUDE

IGNORE NEEDLE.

Map Corrected for Declination

1: Lines are drawn on the map that correspond to magnetic north.

2: Take a bearing by pointing the direction-of-travel line at the object and turning the case until the orienting arrow aligns with the needle. Read the bearing where the direction-of-travel line intersects the dial.

3: Mark your position. Place a side of the baseplate on your position, with the transparent case over a magnetic north line. The direction-of-travel line should be toward the object.

4: Turn the entire compass by the baseplate (do not rotate the case!) until the orienting arrow is parallel to the magnetic north line. Ignore the needle.

5: Draw a line along the baseplate from your position toward the object. You will probably have to extend this line with a ruler for it to cross an object on the map that is similar to the one you see in the field.

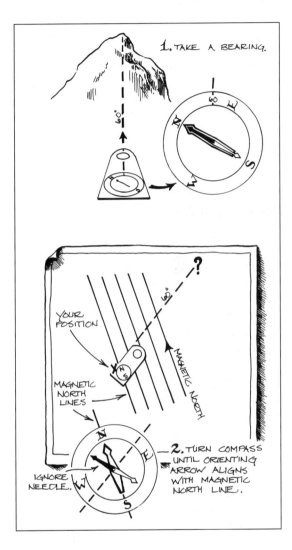

1. TAKE A BEARING.

YOUR POSITION

MAGNETIC NORTH LINES

MAGNETIC NORTH

IGNORE NEEDLE.

2. TURN COMPASS UNTIL ORIENTING ARROW ALIGNS WITH MAGNETIC NORTH LINE.

A Bearing from a Mapped Object

Lines of Position

Let's say you can't find your position on the map, but you see a landmark in the distance whose position you can pinpoint.

If you were to take a bearing of the landmark and draw it on the map, you could be sure you'd be *somewhere* on that line. What you have drawn is a line of position, a line of sight upon which you're positioned in relation to an object. This may seem to provide very little information about your position, but in fact it eliminates everything except that one line—which is quite a lot. And, as we'll soon see, by crossing one line of position with another you can find your *exact* location.

Since you don't know your position, you must take a back bearing (described earlier) to give you the direction from the object toward you. A back bearing is the reciprocal, or opposite, of a normal, or direct, bearing. It's 180 degrees different. Once taken, it is corrected for declination and then drawn from the object on the map.

Compass Corrected for Declination

1: The compass's declination adjustment is set to correspond with geographic north.
2: Take a back bearing by pointing the direction-of-travel line at the object and turning the case until the orienting arrow aligns with the South (not the North!) end of the needle. Read the back bearing where the direction-of-travel line intersects the dial.
3: Place a side of the baseplate on the point that represents the object on the map, with the pivot over a geographic north line such as a left- or right-hand border or a drawn-in line of longitude. The direction-of-travel line should be toward where you think you are.
4: Turn the entire compass by the baseplate (do not rotate the case!) until North and South on the dial (not the orienting arrow or lines!) is parallel to the geographic north line. Ignore the needle.
5: A line drawn along the baseplate toward you from the object is your line of position. You will probably have to extend this line with a ruler.

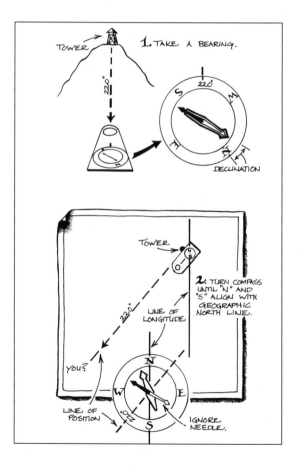

Map Corrected for Declination

1: Lines are drawn on the map that correspond to magnetic north.
2: Take a back bearing by pointing the direction-of-travel line at the object and turning the case until the orienting arrow is aligned with the South (not the North!) end of the needle. Read the back bearing where the direction-of-travel line intersects the dial.
3: Place a side of the baseplate on the point that represents the object on the map, with the transparent case over a magnetic north line. The direction-of-travel line should point toward where you think you are.
4: Turn the entire compass by the baseplate (do not rotate the case!) until the orienting arrow is parallel to the magnetic north line. Ignore the needle.
5: A line drawn along the baseplate toward you from the object is your line of position. You will probably have to extend this line with a ruler.

TOWER

1. TAKE A BEARING.

240°

240

TOWER

2. TURN COMPASS UNTIL ORIENTING ARROW ALIGNS WITH MAGNETIC NORTH LINE.

MAGNETIC NORTH

240°

YOU?

LINE OF POSITION

IGNORE NEEDLE.

Other Lines of Position

In the previous section we used a compass bearing to give us a line of position, a line of sight in relation to a known object. But there are other lines of position as well, and for most you don't even need a compass. By studying a map and using a bit of imagination you'll see that there are lines of position all around you. You're probably standing on or next to one right now.

The most accurate and easy-to-use lines of position are naturally occurring transits. When two objects in the field line up one behind the other, they form a transit. And a line drawn on the map connecting the two objects would make a perfect line of position with you somewhere on it. A careful look at the map will show a wealth of transits, because almost any two mapped and identifiable objects will do. Find them on the map, draw a line through their two points, and extend the line toward your general area. When you see those two points in the field line up, you are on that line. It's simple and precise.

The "line" in a line of position can be circular as well as straight. If you know how far it is to an object (a skill you'll learn later in this book), you can use that distance as the radius of a circle with the object at its center. You must be somewhere on this circle of position.

Lines of position can also be curved or irregular. Any trail, road, firebreak, ridge, powerline, stream, lake shore, or railroad track is a potential line of position. As long as it's a linear feature that can be found on a map, it qualifies as a line of position.

It's fortunate that there are so many different types of lines of position because, as we'll see on page 104, crossing any two or more of them can give us our exact position on the map. The opportunities are all around us.

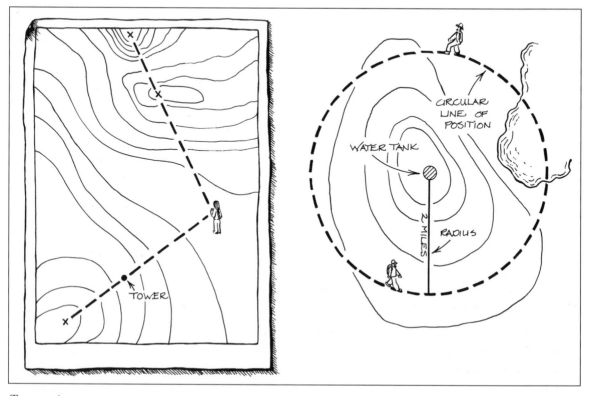

Two transits.

Warning Bearings

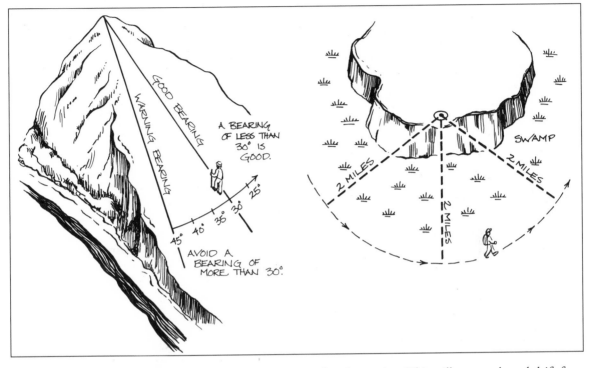

Lines of Position for Avoiding Obstacles

Some lines of position, when plotted in advance, can be used to warn of obstacles and keep you out of difficult terrain.

A back bearing drawn from a landmark can form one such a line of position. Draw a line from a mapped object that lies along your course, skirting the edge of any feature (such as a cliff or swamp) you want to avoid. This line of position is your warning bearing—an invisible barrier over which you don't want to cross.

Draw a second bearing that stands off from the obstacle with a good margin for error. This is the bearing you will walk along. Note the difference between the two bearings, and whether the bearings increase or decrease toward the obstacle. This tells you that you can stray either higher or lower than a particular course and still keep clear. As you travel, continue to check your compass bearing on the landmark until you are sure you have passed

the obstruction. This will prevent lateral drift from setting you onto it.

Circular lines of position, as described on the previous page, can also be used to keep you away from terrain you wish to avoid. By drawing a circle around such an area you create an avoidance circle on the map. To keep outside this circle, you'll need to estimate how far away you are from the object of the circle's center. This technique, adapted from marine navigation, is not often useful to hikers because rolling terrain affords few opportunities for accurate distance estimates.

But it's nice to know nevertheless.

Crossing Lines of Position

The Fix

While you were napping in the back of Miss Laurel's geometry class, you might have missed the axiom: "Two straight lines can intersect at only one point." It was something to yawn at back then, but it's a perfect definition of what happens when you cross two lines of position. You get a fix, the only spot on the map where you could be.

A single line of position narrows your location to a long, pencil-thin line. But where are you on that line? It's impossible to tell unless you cross it with another line of position. Like two bearings making an intersection in the wilderness, you are at their junction.

Consider the analogy of being lost while trying to find a friend's house. You call her and say, "I'm on Constitution Avenue." That's one line of position. Then you add, "Where it meets 15th Street." Now you've crossed your first line of position with another. You've provided a positive fix. You're one-third of a mile south-southeast of the White House in Washington, DC. She'd be able to find you.

In the field, you take back bearings of at least two objects, draw lines on the map outward from their positions, and see where the lines cross. In theory, that's where you are, but in reality it is only an approximation. The best bearings most of us are capable of taking are within one degree of accuracy, and more often closer to two or three degrees in error. After a mile, an error like that turns bearing "lines" into a sizable wedge. It is therefore safest to consider crossed position lines not so much a fix as an area of probability.

To reduce this area, lines of position should intersect at 90 degrees, or as close to a right angle as possible. Angles of less 60 or more than 120 degrees should be avoided. Accuracy can be improved by using nearby objects, and three bearings are always better than two. Indeed, the more bearings the better, assuming all are plotted carefully.

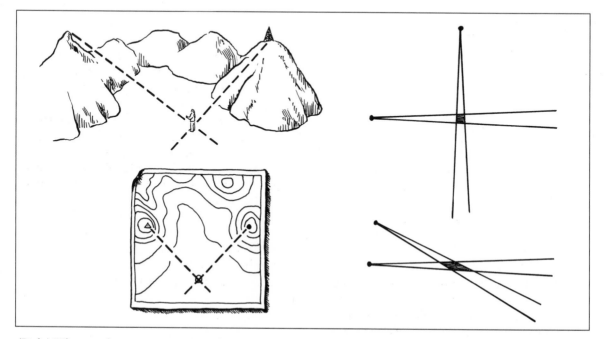

(Right) When two bearings cross at an angle near 90 degrees (top) you get a close read (shaded area) of your position. A poor crossing angle (bottom) yields a sloppy position estimate.

Returning to the Same Spot

A Fix in Reverse

You've found a hidden cave with the Holy Grail in it. Good for you. But in order to dig it out, you have to go back to town for a shovel and some lunch. Rather than risk losing the treasure again for another few thousand years, you take bearings of at least two landmarks to get a fix. Three bearings would be better. You could then mark the spot accurately on your map and return to it anytime you liked.

But, alas, you do not have a map. All you have is your compass. Well, it's not as bad as you thought. You can still relocate the cave by finding the one spot where those bearings cross.

To return, retrace your steps as best you can until you see one of your landmarks. Then line yourself up on one of the bearings you noted. That is your main highway back. Walk along that bearing toward the landmark until you can take a bearing of the second mark. Continue walking along the first bearing until the second bearing matches what it was originally. When the two (or three) bearings match the ones you originally took, you're back in the same spot.

As you'll soon see, this procedure is a variant of the baseline method, particularly when used with a bearing, as described in the next chapter.

This system works for relocating good fishing spots in the middle of a lake or your camp in the middle of nowhere. In unfamiliar terrain, it's a good idea to take a starting fix on your trailhead, so you can find your way back out should plans go awry. The only thing you must do is make a careful note of those landmarks and bearings, because you aren't going to remember them.

A Running Fix

There may be times when you want to fix your position but have only one mapped landmark from which to take a bearing. Since a fix is obtained by crossing at least two lines of position, your situation might seem hopeless—unless you know how to take a running fix. This skill requires that you proceed on a straight course and can measure the distance you've covered. The latter is something we'll learn later in this chapter. Meanwhile, here are two useful forms of running fixes:

Two Bearings and a Run

Take a back bearing from an object and plot it on the map. Now walk a straight course until the bearing has changed by at least 30 degrees. Take a second bearing and draw that on the map. Estimate the distance you traveled (see instructions later in this chapter) between the two bearings. Using the map's bar scale, mark the distance on the edge of a piece of paper or measure it with a ruler. Now align your straight-edge parallel to your course and spanning the two bearing lines, and slide it out along the bearings (keeping it parallel to your course) until the distance traveled just fits between the bearing lines. The points of intersection indicate your positions at the times you took the two bearings. Use the last one as your fix. It won't be precise, but it will be close.

Doubling the Bearing

This gives you your distance from an object, whether it's on the map or not, by taking two bearings while walking along a straight course. When you take your first bearing, note how many degrees it differs from your course. This difference is the relative bearing to the object. Hold a straight course and keep taking bearings until you get one that is exactly double the first. If, for example, the first relative bearings was 30 degrees, the second should be 60 degrees. You don't need to plot either of these bearings on the map.

Now estimate the distance you traveled between the two bearings. That, through the magic of geometry, is also the present distance between you and the object. If the object is mapped, you can draw the second bearing on your map, mark on it the known distance from the object—and you have a fix.

The only conditions are that the first bearing must be no more than 45 degrees or no less than 10 degrees. Angles of less than 10 degrees introduce a chance for error.

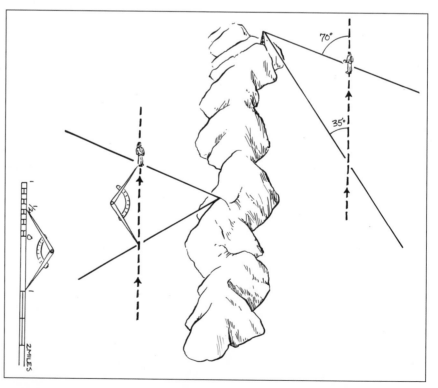

Finding Distance Off

Knowing your distance from something, when you don't know where you are, can put you back on the map.

If you are on a line of position (a bearing, transit, or any linear feature) and can tell how far you are from a mapped object that is also on that line, you can define where you are in relation to it.

As we've already seen, finding the distance to (or from) something can also give you a circle of position to help keep you oriented, or an avoidance circle to keep you clear of difficult terrain. Then too, knowing the distance and how long it will take to get to a destination will be of great help in planning your day. Distance-off measurements are more often useful to sea kayakers and lake paddlers than to hikers. Nevertheless, these techniques find occasional use on land as well, and are fun to know.

The most accurate way of measuring distance is with a rangefinder, an expensive piece of gadgetry you're not likely to have. In its place we can use some primitive, but surprisingly reliable, techniques.

Estimating Distance by Eye

With some practice, estimating distance by eye can do the job nicely. But the eye can be deceived.

Things often appear closer when:

- You're looking up or down a hill at them.
- They're brightly illuminated.
- They're seen across water, snow, or flat sand.
- Atmospheric conditions are clear.

Things often appear farther away when:

- The light is poor.
- Their color blends with the background.
- They are over uneven ground.
- Your vision is channeled, as, for example, down a road or valley.

We shall not cease from exploration
And the end of all our exploring
Will be to arrive where we started
And know the place for the first time.

—Four Quartets
T.S. Eliot

To estimate distance, use the following as a guide. Try it for yourself when you know how far off things really are. See what they look like, and remember that as a reference.

Six miles—Large houses, small apartment buildings, and towers can be recognized.

Two miles—Chimneys stand out; windows are dots; vehicles can be seen moving.

One mile—People look like dots; trunks of large trees can be seen.

One-half mile—People look like posts; larger branches on trees become visible.

One-quarter mile—Head and body forms, leg movement, and colors of clothing become discernible.

250 yards—Faces and hands are blurs but can be seen, as can details on clothing.

100 yards—Eyes appear as dots.

50 yards—Eyes and mouth can clearly be seen.

Finding Distance Off

Finger Angles

This requires you to know an object's height, or
the width separating two points. You then hold
your fingers at arm's length to measure the angle
between the object's base and top (for height), or
between two points (for width). Enter that angle
and the known height or width into the formula
to get distance off. Since the height of a particular
feature or object is rarely noted on maps, you'll
more often use the distance between two points.
Look for mountain peaks, two ends of a cliff, two
ends of an island, bridge abutments, or any horizontal separation that can be accurately measured
on a map.

Distance Off by Winking

You can also measure an angle by winking, using
the ten-to-one rule. With one eye closed, hold a
finger at arm's length next to one point. Then
close that eye and open the other to look at the
same finger.

Now estimate to the best of your ability the
distance, in miles or yards, that your finger
appeared to jump sideways from the first point.

Multiply your estimate by ten—and that's how
far you are from the point. Roughly, anyway.

On many occasions you won't be able to cover
a whole length with one wink. But that's all right.
Try estimating. On a 500-foot-wide island, did
your wink get you halfway across, or one-third of
the way?

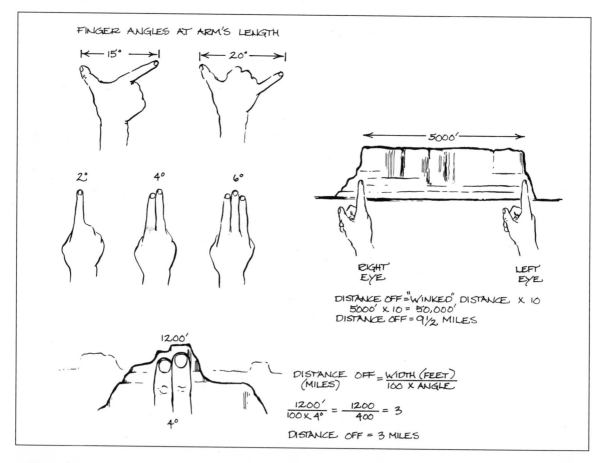

Finding Distance Off

How Far to the Horizon?

This can come in handy when traveling over open terrain, on larger lakes, or any other place where you have an unobstructed view of the horizon. If you see something sitting just on the edge of the earth's curve (the horizon), and know your elevation, you'll be able to tell how far off it is. This technique won't work when the terrain between you and the horizon is anything but perfectly flat.

To determine your elevation, look at the map's contour lines. If you're on a boat, by the shore of a lake, or on a flat open plain, you need only know the height of your eye above the flat surface between you and the horizon. The higher up you are, the farther away your horizon is. By taking the square root of your elevation (or height) in feet you'll find just how far away that is in miles.

This is, in fact, a simplification of a more complex formula, but it's accurate enough. The only hard part is finding the square root, but as this is only a rough estimation at best, the simplest way to find the square root is to multiply a number by itself until you get close to your elevation. A couple of good guesses (or, of course, a calculator) should do it.

If you'll be looking out at the world from a consistent height, as you do when seated in a canoe, you can measure the height of your eye above the water, and figure the square root of this accurately at home. From then on, you'll always know how far it is to the water horizon.

If you want to know how far it is to an object that lies beyond the horizon, you'll have to make allowance for the extra distance involved.

For example, you'll see the top of a bold headland long before you see its base, meaning that it is farther away than your horizon. To find out just how far, you'll have to figure in the headland's height as well as your own.

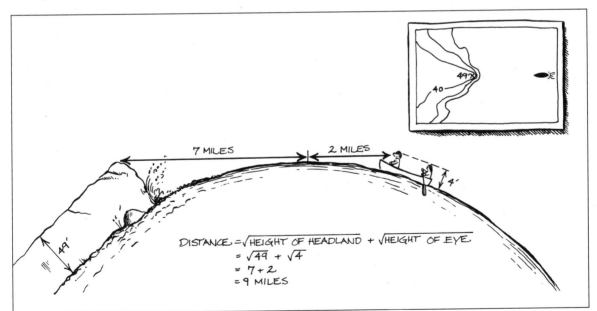

$$\text{DISTANCE} = \sqrt{\text{HEIGHT OF HEADLAND}} + \sqrt{\text{HEIGHT OF EYE}}$$
$$= \sqrt{49} + \sqrt{4}$$
$$= 7 + 2$$
$$= 9 \text{ MILES}$$

Measuring Distance Covered

To help plan your journey, you need to know how much ground you can cover within the time available. Once underway, you'll need even more precise distance information so you can track your progress along a trail, find your position on the map, or estimate how far you still have to go.

Your goal is to measure distance covered accurately. To do this you can use your stride, the distance you span in a step. It's reasonably consistent and therefore useful for measurement. To make things simpler, we'll use your double-stride, the distance covered between every second step, or each time your right (or left) foot comes down. This is usually about five feet. To check, walk a measured course of at least 500 feet at a your normal pace and stride while counting each time your right (or left) foot touches the ground.

Divide the distance walked by the count to find how far you go with every two steps. This is also a good time to see how many minutes it takes to cover a mile (5,280 feet). Armed with this information you can now measure how far you travel by counting the number of steps you take. If each double-stride is five feet, then after 200 steps you've gone a thousand feet. Granted, it's a mind-deadening task, but it can be done. Roman soldiers did it. For them, every thousand (or "mille") double-steps became the unit of measure known as a mile. Of course, the stride you measured was under ideal conditions, but it's a good standard that can be modified to suit conditions.

A practical way of counting is to start with a pocketful of pebbles. After each 100 double-strides, shift a pebble to another pocket. To get the distance covered, count the pebbles and multiply by a hundred. Multiply that in turn by the length of your stride.

It's about as much fun as filing your taxes. In addition, you wind up with dirt in your pockets. So you may be tempted to buy a pedometer to do the job. But don't waste your money. Even the new high-tech ones are good only on firm, level ground. As soon as you start climbing over fallen trees, jumping from rock to rock, or scrambling down loose sand, the gadget becomes useless.

It is easier for most people to use time as a measure of distance. Easier, because our internal rhythm or pulse gives us a natural sense for it. You can probably judge the time of day, or how long you've been doing something, without looking at a clock. With practice many of us can come to within ten minutes of estimating the correct time from the last sunrise or sunset—which is pretty good.

How far can you go in a given time? Back in 1892, W. Naismith, a Scottish mountaineer, came up with the following rule:

"An hour for every 3 miles on the map, with an additional hour for every 2,000 feet of ascent."

That works out to 20 minutes per mile on an easy trail with no pack, which is probably only feasible for an athletic hiker on level terrain. Most people can only average 2 miles per hour (30 minutes per mile) under good conditions without constant hurrying. With a full pack, or on a difficult trail, this can increase to at least 40 minutes per mile, and a full pack on a tough trail will push your time up to 60 minutes. The variables are endless. Marshy or rough terrain, thick undergrowth, dense woods, altitude, fatigue, snow or rain, extreme heat or cold, wind, darkness, and pack weight all take their toll. You also lose speed on descents as well as ascents, although only about half as much. And groups of hikers move slower than solo hikers.

Use these estimates as a route-planning guide. Study the map, draw slope profiles, or figure out slope gradients. A hike that measures 15 miles on the flat map and ascends 4,000 feet in the real world will take about nine hours nonstop, and you'd need at least an extra hour for rest stops. That's a reasonable estimate. You'll find, though, that distances to be covered tend to be underestimated before starting out, and distances traveled are overestimated when walking them. To work out your rate of progress, measure elapsed times and distances covered whenever you can. Write these figures down for use later when all you have is your sense of time and a few pebbles in your pocket.

Dead Reckoning

There may come a time when landmarks and points of reference are few and far between, or so indistinguishable as to be confusing. It could happen on the plains of Nebraska, Alaska's tundra, or while canoeing a large lake—anyplace where there seems to be nothing to work with. It could even happen in familiar territory in bad visibility. This situation will force you to stop navigating by eye and begin finding your way by intellect.

The technique used by mariners is called *dead reckoning*—an unfortunate combination of words. But don't be thrown off; the "dead" comes from "ded.," a contraction of deduced. It's not a reference to a style of navigation practiced on the River Styx. This is position-finding by deduction. You work out where you are in relation to a previously known point by using distances and directions traveled from it.

Using Map and Compass

You begin your journey from a positive fix, a point you are sure of and can locate on the map. From there you maintain accurate records of dis-

tance and direction for each leg of your route. You then use these records to update your position on the map.

Here's an example. You want to go for a walk around a ranch with flat terrain. Starting from a spot you can pick out on the map (say, where a powerline crosses a road), pick a compass heading and follow it. Count steps or use some other method of measuring the distance you walk. When you decide to change direction, stop. Take out the map and draw a course line out from the starting point in the direction you walked. Measure a distance on that line equal to the distance you traveled. That is where you are now—your dead-reckoning, or DR, position. If you do the same each time you change direction, you'll always know where you are, greatly reducing your chances of becoming buzzard bait.

In theory, dead reckoning works. It also works in reality, but maybe not as well as we'd like. Since it is impossible to walk an absolutely straight compass course, and since our techniques for measuring distance are not inherently precise, dead-reckoning positions are always a little suspect. This is why any position derived by this method is referred to as an estimated position, which it very well is.

For short distances, such as a few miles, the cumulative errors are acceptable. But going all day without a secure fix would be flirting with disorientation. Luckily, though, these times will be exceedingly rare unless you're crossing the Greenland ice cap or paddling Lake Superior. Under ordinary circumstances, dead reckoning is merely an interim measure to put you within sight of the next landmark. It's a good way of not getting lost, as long as you accept its limits. Don't be fooled by a cross on a map where your DR position shows you to be. You are more than likely not at that point, just somewhere near it. Dead reckoning does no more than narrow down the area of uncertainty.

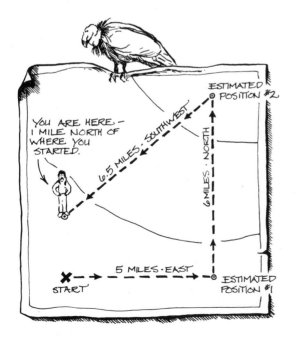

YOU ARE HERE—
I MILE NORTH OF
WHERE YOU
STARTED.

6.5 MILES · SOUTHWEST

6 MILES · NORTH

ESTIMATED POSITION #2

5 MILES · EAST

START

ESTIMATED POSITION #1

Using Compass Only

You can, if necessary, find your way home at the end of almost any journey by compass alone. It is always better to work with both map and compass together, but if you find yourself with only a compass all is not lost.

The key is to divide your outward journey into straight-line legs. Start by following a compass course until you need to turn. At that point stop, write down the time it took to get there and the direction you traveled in. Then head off on the new course, noting your new direction and how long it takes to get to the next turning point. Each time you change direction, write down the new course and the time it took to get from the previous turning point. Continue doing this throughout your journey. When you finally decide to head back, you can either retrace your steps or make a beeline directly for home.

Going back the way you came is a simple matter of reading your records in reverse order and converting compass courses to their reciprocals (180 degrees different from those you followed on the way out). But covering the same ground is boring, and it's often a longer route home. A better way is to make a straight run back. This is done by taking your records and converting them into a "chart," a scaled-down graphic representation of each leg of your trip that is correct for time traveled (distance) and compass courses walked (direction).

It can be done with paper and pencil, or lines drawn in the dirt. Starting anywhere you like, draw each leg to scale. The end of the last leg represents your present position. From this chart, you can now find the direction back to your starting point, and then follow that direction on the compass. This doesn't give you your position on a map relative to your surroundings, so you really don't know where you are. But that doesn't matter. You do know where you are in relation to home and safety—which is just fine.

The main advantage of this system over dead reckoning with a map is that distances are mea-sured in time—not feet, yards, or miles. There's no need for accurate distance measurements, which are hard to make while walking. And there's no need to bother with declination conversions. Everything relates to the compass's magnetic north.

This type of dead reckoning was once common on ships at sea, using traverse boards to note courses, distances, and changes in both. Nineteenth-century European explorers in Africa used a similar technique, and recently Don Paul, an ex-Green Beret, has modified it into a complete system of navigation.

All you have to do is record compass courses for each leg and the time spent on them. Then you make a chart from your records. Here's how to make the chart:

1: Find a flat open piece of ground, the bigger the better.
2: Pick a spot to represent your starting point. Mark it with a stick in the ground.
3: Plot direction for the first leg. From your records, find the compass course you traveled and duplicate that on your chart. If you walked toward 40 degrees, lay the compass on the ground and draw a line in the dirt 40 degrees out from the stick representing your starting point.
4: Plot distance for the first leg. From your records find the time it took to walk the first leg. Pick a scale to represent time. The length of your shoe could equal ten minutes, or a handspan could equal five minutes. The unit of measurement is unimportant, but consistency is: Whatever unit you choose, you must stick with it for the whole chart. Measure out the time traveled along the course line of your first leg, and mark that spot with a stone.
5: Plot the direction and time for all subsequent legs as you did for the first.
6: At the end of the last leg, place a stick in the ground. That is your current position. Lay the compass on the ground and take the

bearing of the stick representing your point of departure. That bearing is your direct compass course home.

Unfortunately, this method will not work in mountainous country. Walking times vary too much going up and down steep slopes, therefore making "distances" on your chart inaccurate. It works best where the land is fairly flat.

Refer to time in your notes by the military 24-hour clock system. Remember when subtracting one time from another that there are 60 minutes in an hour, not 100. If you start at 1440 and stop at 1510, you find the difference between the two by subtracting 1440 from 1510, which is 0030 (30 minutes). Be careful. With ordinary numbers, 1,510 minus 1,440 would be 70. But minutes and seconds of time, like minutes and seconds of degrees, are based on the number 60. Incidentally,

recording elapsed time is much easier with a stopwatch.

For this kind of dead reckoning to work satisfactorily, you must walk only in straight lines. While you'll find few straight paths in nature, you can break down almost any curve into a series of short straight lines.

Keeping a uniform pace (walking speed) is important because it affects time. When your speed changes, record it. If you break out of some thick underbrush onto an open field, stop and record it as a new leg, even if your course remains the same.

The bigger the chart, the fewer the chances of making errors and getting angles wrong.

Like map-and-compass dead reckoning, this type is not absolutely precise, but done carefully, it gets you close. In most cases, that's enough.

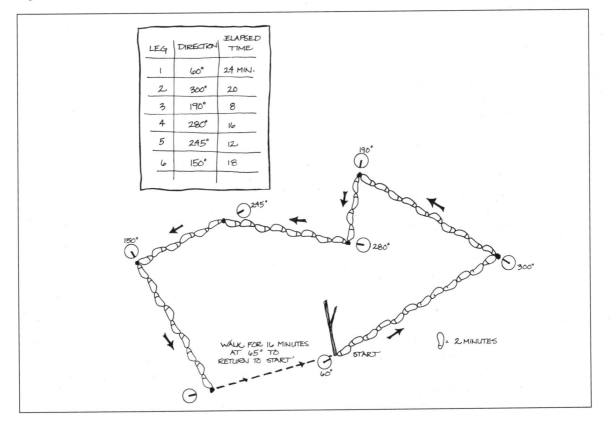

LEG	DIRECTION	ELAPSED TIME
1	60°	24 MIN.
2	300°	20
3	190°	8
4	280°	16
5	245°	12
6	150°	18

WALK FOR 16 MINUTES AT 65° TO RETURN TO START

START

🐾 = 2 MINUTES

Chapter Five
NAVIGATION IN USE

What you learned in the previous chapter was about the mechanics of navigation. While technique is important, it must not be thought of as the culmination of, or a replacement for, the basic tenets of wayfinding described in the beginning of this book. Don't let the comforting mechanics of using map and compass lull you into complacency. The good navigator needs and employs everything available when out in the field. For there is much more to finding your way than lines on a map or bearings from a compass. As you travel, think of what you and the world around you would look like to a bird overhead. Envision the larger picture and your place in it. This is your mental map. Compare it with what you see and what you find on the map in your hands. Do this by continually updating your position through the use of sequential landmarks, or by keeping track of how far and in what directions you have gone. Above all, stay aware of the world you are moving through. Consider navigation not so much as a technique, but a habit of thought, a practice of awareness of the land, its indicators, and what is going on around you.

At the heart of navigating are three questions: Where am I? Where am I going? How do I get there? Simple questions, requiring thoughtful answers. Answers that can be found with a map, compass, and the ability to discover and decipher clues.

Develop all your navigational abilities and trust them, yet remain skeptical and willing to question your judgment. When you can, confirm your observations. Always be sure of where you are, where you are going, and how you will get there.

Let's recap the basic tenets we've learned so far:

- No one has an innate sense of direction. So don't trust yours, trust your compass instead.
- You are not capable of walking in a straight line over long distances without the aid of external clues.
- Most of the directional guides found in nature are unreliable on their own, needing legitimate map-and-compass work to reinforce them.
- A compass and a map will not get you there or back without skill and effort.
- You can't start navigating when you first feel lost. It must be done from the start.
- When lost, there is no assurance that others will find you. Do what you can to avoid getting lost. If it happens, do what you can to help others find you.

Route Planning

Before you head into the wilderness, it's wise to do some pre-trip planning. Begin by studying on your map the character of the region you will be traversing and how it affects your choice of routes. Locate your starting point and your objective, then try "walking" an imaginary straight line between the two. It may be the most direct route, but is it the quickest or easiest? Listen to what the map tells you. Note the vegetation, ground surface, and slope gradients. Are the contour lines along your route too close together? Rather than scrambling up and down, would it take less effort to follow a single contour line? It might be a longer journey, but you'd stay at one level. Seek out potential obstacles. A map gives a bird's-eye view of what's around and ahead of you. Use it. Pick out potential landmarks and good baselines to aim for. Plan your route in short segments. Consider the difficulty of the terrain and how far you will realistically want to travel. This is also a good time to consider potential campsites.

After selecting a route, highlight it with a felt-tipped marker pen to make it stand out from the jumble of other lines. On straight stretches, write the compass courses toward and away (in case you have to backtrack) from your objective, and the distance traveled between course changes. The route you choose now need not be considered final. Things often look different on the trail—you can't know everything from a map. But at least you are heading out with a plan from which intelligent choices can be made.

Use maps to take in the big picture and see beyond the narrow path of your travels. An extra-small-scale map covering a greater area than your large-scale navigational map can be helpful for this. Look for prominent yet distant landmarks to use for bearings. Be aware of main roads and towns, and their locations and directions relative to your route. This may come in handy when emergencies occur. You might even find at this point that a map of an adjacent quadrant would be handy. Maps are relatively cheap at the store, but priceless when they are needed—but unavailable—in the field.

Consider your route back as well. The most straightforward way to return is along the path that takes you in. It may not be as interesting as a different return route, yet it may be necessary if the weather turns. Cover all your options.

Guidebooks or trail guides are an excellent source of information about trails, camps, regulations, and all the nuances a map cannot portray. Check them for their latest revision dates, and try to avoid outdated editions. If the guide is too cumbersome to take along, transfer as much information as you can to the map. Note things like shelters, drinking water sources, trail conditions, and changes made after your map's revision date. Explore other sources of information. Seek out rangers and those whose job it is to know what is going on, but be wary of the ever-present local "expert."

File a travel plan before leaving, giving a written itinerary to someone responsible. List the name of every person in your party, the telephone numbers of friends or relatives, where you are leaving your car, what gear you are carrying, where you're headed, your intended route, likely campsites, time of departure, the estimated time and place of your return, and any anticipated side trips. Make sure you give the names and numbers of authorities to call if you are overdue (rangers, rescue groups).

Finally, make sure that when you return safely, you immediately contact the person with whom you left your travel plan. If you don't, rescuers may unnecessarily risk their lives looking for you.

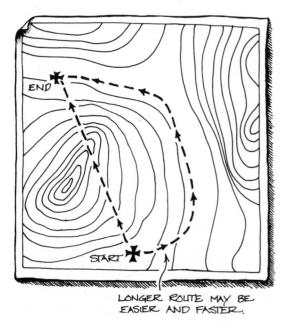

LONGER ROUTE MAY BE EASIER AND FASTER.

The Practice of Navigation

Navigation is more state of mind than set procedures. To keep track of your position, you must stay alert and look for opportunities to use a wide variety of techniques. As the land changes, so should your approach to wayfinding.

Effective navigation requires imagination. It draws on all your skills, utilizing the mind as well as the senses. By all means hone your map-and-compass abilities, while at the same time never straying from the rules of basic wayfinding.

When traveling, try to picture your surroundings as if you were looking down from an airplane. Compare this image to what you see around you and what you find on the map. Most important, watch where you are going, and practice total awareness of the indicators around you.

That is the general philosophy of navigation. Now here are some specifics:

Orient the map (align it to the landscape) with your compass before referring to it. The printing may be upside down or at an angle, but it will be easier to correlate what you see with what is on the map. This will help you choose the correct fork at a junction, or the correct direction on a mountain descent.

Strive to know where you are on the map at all times, and the direction in which you are heading. Don't wait until you get an uneasy feeling that you are not 100 percent sure.

Continually update your position through the use of landmarks or by keeping track of how far and in what directions you have traveled. In reality, it is rare to know precisely where you are at every moment. Typically, we leave a known location, pass through areas and intervals of relative uncertainty as to our exact whereabouts, then reestablish an accurate position at every opportunity. The alternating pattern of pinpoint locations and areas of probability continues until we reach our destination.

The navigator's objective is to restrict the times of ambiguity to a minimum and to keep the areas of uncertainty down to a circle of a few hundred yards (rather than a few miles). Do this by frequently checking your position.

Every time you reach a landmark, junction, or fork in the trail, or when you break clear from the woods so you can see the surrounding terrain, confirm your position on the map. Or, discipline yourself to stop every twenty minutes to keep a running track of where you might be. Even if you can't ascertain your exact position on these "navbreaks," you will at least be reducing your area of uncertainty.

Though it's usually impractical and thus rarely done, you can do yourself a favor when bushwacking or traveling cross country by keeping a running log (notes) or a sketch map of your route. "Turned to 275 degrees at mouth of pocket canyon. Walked eleven minutes to dry stream bed. Followed stream bed north for nine minutes, turned off to 90 degrees facing distant butte . . ."

Upon leaving major turning points or landmarks, write down (on the map, next to their position) the time of day. This will help you judge your pace and the distance you're covering. Turn around and look back at every junction, change of direction, or landmark. Study where you came from, the way it looks, and any prominent features. This is what you will see on the return trip. Get to know it now so it will look familiar when you see it again.

Be willing to question your judgment. Keep an open mind and observe objectively, then determine or confirm your position. Do not choose your position on the map first and then make the world conform to it.

Impartially evaluate your judgment by comparing input from a variety of navigational techniques.

Accept that you cannot hold a compass course of better than four degrees and that lateral drift may be occurring. By all means try to prevent this, but make allowance for this possibility when estimating your position.

Use intermediate landmarks when following a compass course, making a number of short legs rather than one long run. This will lessen the potential for confusion and disorientation.

Check the map for likely baselines lying across

your route. Always aim for a large target and then use it to lead you toward your objective. Utilize the practice, described earlier, of aiming to one side of your destination. More details are given later in this chapter under the heading "Aiming Off."

Think of navigating toward an objective as constantly narrowing down areas of possibility. Use coarse navigation to get you into the general vicinity, then ever-increasing precision to search out your goal. It's like driving in a city you don't know. You take an interstate to the city, then a main avenue to the neighborhood, locate the right street, then find the block and house. Each choice gets you closer to your destination.

Study the map for a prominent feature near your destination, something that can be easily reached, located, and identified. Head toward that first, then start your precision navigation from there.

Choose landmarks that will not be obscured, or if they are, only intermittently. Try to keep your goal and starting point in sight. Barring that ideal situation, keep at least one landmark in sight at all times.

Maintain a point or line of reference. Ideally this would be something that is always visible, such as a ridge. If not, use something whose existence is confirmed by the map—for example, a road running parallel to your route, but a quarter-mile away. Locate yourself and your route in terms of direction toward and distance from this reference.

Don't feel you must use every landmark. Just keep track of the more obvious features beyond your immediate route, while concentrating on the finer details along your path.

As much as possible, stick to your chosen route. This way, even if you can't find your destination, you'll be able to retrace your steps.

Never depend on your sense of direction, a "feeling," or a hunch. Base all decisions on facts. Be opportunistic. Make use of all your observational and navigation skills.

On the Trail

You wouldn't think there'd be a need for navigation on a trail. But you start walking—expecting something like a freeway with well-marked exits—and, well, somehow you blunder off into trouble.

As you may have noticed, trails have little in common with highways, which is why more people get lost on trails than you'd expect. Every exit on a highway is an opportunity to pinpoint your position; every intersection on a poorly marked trail is a chance to choose wrong without realizing it.

Even on a well-worn trail, it makes sense to know where you are. Usually the only compass work you'll need to do will be when orienting the map. From then on it becomes a matter of keeping track of consecutive landmarks, relating your movement to references, and remembering distances and directions traveled. Try to maintain a running record in your mind of the path you have followed. If the route has been circuitous, keep a written log (notes) or make a simple sketch map. Both are good for finding your position and a route back.

Trails offer the easiest path from A to B. You'll definitely stand a better chance of not getting misplaced by following a trail and straying from it only when you are absolutely sure you know where you are on the map, and when you have a planned route to your destination. Be aware, however, that in many wilderness areas you are requested to stay on trails for ecological reasons.

Incidentally, don't give up a trail until it either disappears or heads off in a direction that is obviously wrong. When confronted with a situation like this, confirm your position on the map, head back to the last fork or junction, and re-plan your route. Do not set off blindly, bushwhacking in what you assume to be the right direction. There's usually a very good reason why there are no trails where you are headed.

Unfortunately, trails may foster unwarranted confidence. Don't be too sure you won't get disoriented when you leave the trail, or that you'll be able to return to it, no matter what. A trail is just a thin scrape on the land. It's not that easy to identify once you're separated from it. You may say to yourself, "I'm only going to take a brief shortcut, why bother with the map or compass?" But trails have a strange way of disappearing.

Watch out for poorly maintained, old, or marginal-looking trail marks. They could mean you're on a trail to nowhere. It's even possible that they were made by wildlife, and you might not be interested in good forage. Cairns are often built by people who were lost. Markers may also be missing or destroyed. Be suspicious. Be even more suspicious when there are no markers at all.

Maps, too, can be disappointing. Many of the clearly marked trails on your park map, the ones that look so obvious and easy to follow, may in reality be poorly maintained, overgrown, or rudimentary to start with. In large parks or national forests, there may be too many trails for mapmakers to inspect and keep current.

Keep track of where you are so as not to lose your feeling for directions. If your visibility is suddenly limited by thick woods, fog, rain, night, or snow, and the trail "disappears," where do you go? The same can happen on rough terrain, where we tend to watch only where we are stepping—directly ahead of us. This makes it easy to miss a turn or to go off on an unmarked path. As in all navigation, when on the trail—watch where you are going.

Trail markers. Know what they mean, but please refrain from making your own. You might only confuse future hikers.

Hitting What You Aim For

Baselines

Bushwhacking through thickets, traversing sharp inclines, and weaving around trees all test the limits of your ability to hold a precise course. Your compass may be the best there is, and you may use it with great skill, but you could still wind up between four and eight degrees off course after a long trek. In addition to the terrain, factors working against you include the fact that most compasses can't be read to less than one degree, deviation may have gone unnoticed, lateral drift occurred, your sighting technique may be a little sloppy, or an old map may have given you an outdated declination which you, in turn, made errors in applying. Each throws you off by a small amount, but the cumulative error can be substantial.

To offset these limitations, aim for something big. Optimism is laudable, but do not believe that you will always be able to hit what you aim for. Put the odds in your favor by leaving room for error.

One solution is to choose destinations on a *baseline*. This is a long reference line running across your intended course, making it a hard target to miss. A baseline can be as real as a road, stream, coastline, fence, railroad tracks, powerline, ridge, or the steep side of a valley. It can also be an imaginary line, a bearing from a compass.

A map will help you to locate the baselines around you or take note of them as you travel. One of the most commonly used baselines is the road where you leave your car at the trailhead. With a good baseline, you don't even need to keep track of your exact course. If you know the general direction of the baseline, and it's long enough, you can always find it. For example, if you parked your car on a north/south road you could wander away in a generally westward direction and know that all you had to do was head vaguely eastward to hit the road again. No straight courses to follow, and a minimum of compass work.

The only problem is this: When you get to the baseline, which way is your destination?

Aiming Off

Given that you will make mistakes and not be able to hold a precisely accurate course, let your mistakes work for you. Make them purposeful, big, and so far to one side that they are no longer mistakes but deliberate offsets.

If you were to try to hit your target dead-on, but couldn't find it when you arrived at the baseline, you wouldn't know whether to turn to the right or the left. But if you'd made sure that you were a long way off to one side, there would be no mystery. You would know without doubt which way to turn. *Aiming off*, as it is known, is an important technique.

How far off course should you aim to be? Well, the average course error is about three degrees, so aiming off by five degrees to one side of the direct course to the destination should do it. Always

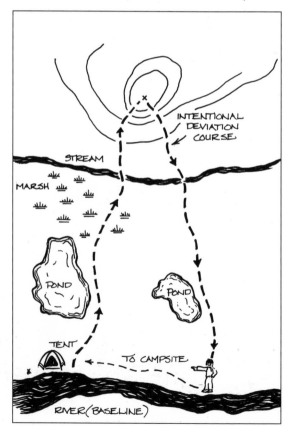

trend toward one side while you're traveling. When you encounter a tree or a rock, go around it toward the side you are aiming for. This way you will always be drifting off to the same side.

Bracketing

Bracketing figuratively encloses your destination by establishing landmarks on either side of it along the baseline. Navigators use this technique as a backup to aiming off.

If you find the baseline close to your destination, and for some reason head off in the wrong direction, you will soon come across a "bracket" telling you to turn back. Your destination is the other way.

Brackets can be existing features; there should be no need to make marks or place flags. They must be far enough apart to encompass even the broadest amount of lateral drift. For example, if you are using a river for a baseline, your brackets could be a dam, rapids, falls, a bridge, a cove, or where a tributary joins. If you have one bracket

upstream of your goal and another downstream, you will be well bracketed and will know which way to turn if and when one is encountered.

If no obvious brackets show up on a map, walk the baseline in each direction. You may find landmarks not shown on the map, Keep notes on what brackets are where. Then, when you're coming back tired and not thinking clearly, you won't have to guess which side the burned tree was on, or the huge boulder. Within the two outer brackets there can be any number of secondary brackets. Record these, too, with a note something like, "Jeep on road. Abandoned shack three-quarter mile to north. Lightning-scarred oak to south, half-mile out. Small pond touches road one mile out."

Bracketing not only tells you in which direction to turn once you reach the line, but also that the line you've reached is the right one. For instance, in areas laced with logging roads you'll know you've hit the right one when you see your brackets. This is particularly helpful to hunters or collectors, who randomly explore an area and do not keep a precise track of their route.

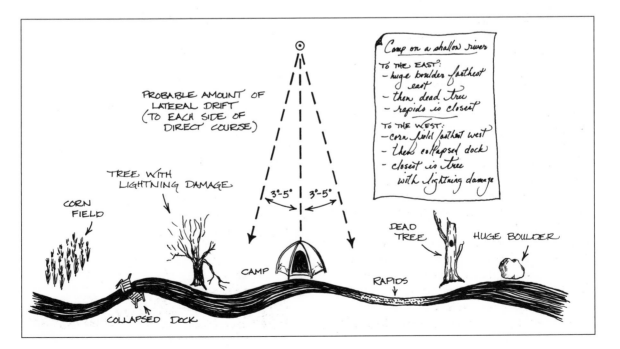

A Bearing as a Baseline

A baseline need not be tangible. It can just as well be an abstract creation such as a compass bearing. Where there are few landmarks, or where they are inconveniently placed, a bearing used as a baseline may be your saviour.

Suppose you are leaving your campsite in the morning and want to be sure you can find it in the afternoon. Take a bearing from your starting point toward a prominent landmark. Write that bearing down; it is now your baseline. Go out and wander around. When you want to return, line yourself up with the landmark so you are on the baseline bearing. Assuming you aimed off toward the landmark, the reciprocal, or back bearing, will be your route home.

This technique isn't limited to a return to your own starting point. Anytime a prominent mapped landmark—say, a peak dominating a valley—will be visible from your destination, you can take its bearing from the map and use that as a baseline.

A bearing of one landmark gives you a baseline. Add a second bearing of another landmark, and you will be able to tell where on that baseline you are.

This is the principle of crossed bearings, which asserts that there is only one spot where two bearings can cross.

In practice, you walk until you are on one bearing, which becomes your baseline. You then take a bearing of the second landmark to determine which direction you should walk on the baseline to make this second bearing match what it should be at your destination. This is the same technique described earlier on how to return to a position established from two bearings.

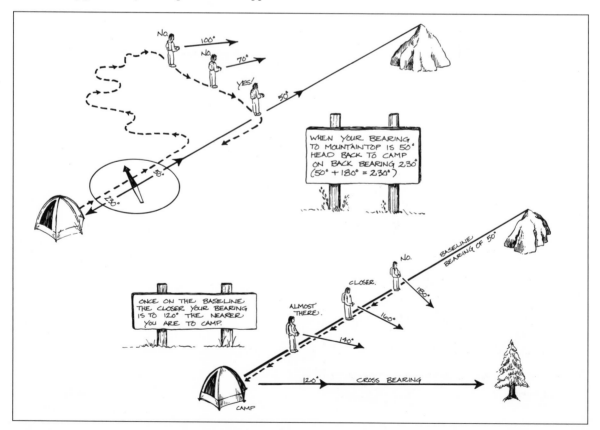

Landmarks as Guides

Handrails and Catch Points

Some landmarks are valuable because they enable you to navigate without a compass, and sometimes even without a map. Let's have a look at the features we call *handrails* and *catch points*:

Handrails.

These are long, natural or man-made features running parallel to your course. They're called handrails because you symbolically latch onto them and follow where they go. The handrail becomes your guide.

A typical handrail would be a fence, a road, the edge of a field, a ridge, a valley, a lake shore, powerlines, or a stream. There's no need to be in actual contact with it. As long as you can maintain a parallel course, the handrail is doing its job.

You can also think of a handrail as a highway. When you find one, you can put your map and compass away for a while and cruise along as if you were on an interstate.

Catch points.

Look on the map for an easily identifiable landmark that shows where to leave the handrail (or highway) and turn onto a new course. These indicators are called catch points, or sometimes collecting features, and tell you it's time to leave the handrail highway. They also confirm your position on the handrail, which, when reached, should be checked on the map.

Almost any mapped feature can be a catch point. And catch points aren't always points either; they can be lines, too, such as a trail crossing your course—which could be used as another handrail. The number of possible handrails and catch points is vast. Look for them. Use them.

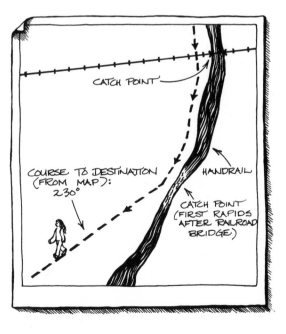

CATCH POINT

COURSE TO DESTINATION (FROM MAP): 230°

HANDRAIL

CATCH POINT (FIRST RAPIDS AFTER RAILROAD BRIDGE)

Sources of Error

We all make mistakes. We simply have to accept that fact. The best we can do is look for them and catch them before they do too much damage. Our instruments make mistakes too, which can induce us to make even greater mistakes of our own.

Here are some common errors we're all likely to commit at one time or another. Look out for:

Map Errors

- Using an old map that has not been recently updated.
- Using maps that have been privately made and printed, which do not adhere to National Map Accuracy Standards. If they do, it will say so on the map.
- Mistaking the plus symbol (+) where lines of latitude and longitude cross for the × symbol (benchmark) and not understanding why you can't locate the benchmark.
- Drawing magnetic-north lines to the angle of the MN arrow on the declination diagram, rather than to the actual declination angle printed next to it.
- Not accounting for annual changes in declination.
- Using directions from a map directly on a compass without adjusting for declination.
- Using a distance-measuring scale on the side of a baseplate compass that does not match the map's scale.
- Inaccurately transferring distance from the bar scale to the map.
- Using a map with a scale too small to show helpful details or give accurate bearings.
- Reading the protractor incorrectly when picking out a direction.
- Failing to correlate the map correctly with your surroundings.

Compass Errors

- Using the north end of the needle to give a bearing instead of the direction-of-travel line or arrow.
- Confusing the north and south ends of the needle. North is usually painted red.
- Overestimating a compass's limits of accuracy (usually between two and four degrees).
- Not taking careful bearings. Always use the same eye when sighting along a compass, and take bearings twice to be sure.
- Overlooking sources of deviation. Compasses are affected by nearby magnetic objects such as radios, knives, belt buckles (even ones that look like brass), cameras, battery-powered watches, guns, overhead powerlines, and railroad tracks. Never place a compass on the hood of a car to do map work.
- Taking directions with a compass and plotting them directly on a map without compensating for declination.
- Using a compass in a magnetic zone other than the one it was intended for.

General Navigation Errors

- Calculating incorrectly when correcting for declination.
- Applying declination in the wrong direction.
- Not recording courses and distances with care and in a manner that will be easily understood.
- Not making many short legs of a long course and not using intermediate landmarks.
- Ignoring the possibility of lateral drift.
- Accepting "local knowledge" without reservation.

When You Are Lost

The day may come when you lose a trail, can't decide which way to go at a junction, or see something that doesn't look right. If you can follow your route back, you are not lost. But if you continue, you could very easily, within an hour or so, become completely lost. This is why you must keep constant track of your position and never charge ahead blindly with hope in your heart (and map and compass buried in your pack).

As soon as you get that slight twinge of uncertainty, stop to get out your map and compass. Retrace your steps in your mind and on the map. Find that last point where you were absolutely positive about your position, and use that as a reference. With the map oriented, look carefully for landmarks and clues around you. If you are becoming nervous or too worried to think clearly, make this nav-break into a rest stop. At this point, the worst that can happen is that you have to walk back the way you came until you are sure of where you are, and then proceed once again from there.

But what happens if you are truly lost? Let's presume you've unknowingly been misreading landmarks and walking the wrong trail for hours without seeing anything wrong. Then the trail stops where it shouldn't. You have convinced yourself all day that what you saw made sense. Now it doesn't. And now you're lost, good and proper.

The first thing to do is stop and admit that you don't know where you are. Don't blunder onward, letting your pride and "sense of direction" take over. Confess your sins so you can begin to undo them.

Fear, with the disbelief, frustration, and panic that accompany it, is the most debilitating result of getting lost. Once it takes hold, you lose your ability to think clearly, see what's around you, and reason objectively. The best way to prevent this is to stop panic before it starts. To calm yourself, remember that at an average speed of perhaps two miles per hour, you can't have strayed too far from the rest of the world. So take off your pack, have a snack, and relax for a while. Sort things out calmly. Let other members in the group know

what's going on, build confidence, and start looking for clues. Most of the time, you will be able to reconstruct your mistakes and figure out how you got to where you are, and from there, how to get back. If not, you'll soon be found by others. (You did leave a travel plan with someone didn't you? No? Well, maybe it won't be so soon, after all.) Records show that most lost hikers are found within two or three days.

Orient the map, ask everyone to recall details of landmarks passed, look for prominent features, use all your senses, and try to piece things together. Do not give in to wishful thinking by hastily identifying what you see, making it fit what you want to see. Be cool, be objective. Think of being lost as starting a jigsaw puzzle; begin by gathering the pieces that make up the border, and work inward. From all your data, draw a circle of possibility on the map, a broad area within which you think you're located. That's the border to your puzzle. It's just an estimate, but it's a start and will help direct your thinking. It also breeds confidence. At least now you're on the map.

Look beyond your circle of possibility for hard-to-miss baselines. A river, highway, lake, anything that will make a giant target you can't miss. In case you can't find exactly where you are, so as to be able to continue your hike, the baseline gives you a way back to help. Just head in its general direction until you hit it. You may not be sure where you are on the baseline, but you have now established a valuable line of position that will soon yield more clues and give you a fix.

By the way, there is an old bit of backwoods lore that says: "If you follow a river downstream it will lead to civilization." Don't believe it. No matter which way you turn, your chances are even.

When nothing seems to be coming together, it's time to start scouting about or retracing your steps—searching the immediate area for trails, markers, or anything that can help. But don't get more lost than you are. You followed some logical route (at least it seemed so at the time) to get where you are, so there is a chance of finding your way back. But if you start wandering aimlessly about, you may lose even this thin thread of connection. You may become not just simply lost, but profoundly lost. And there is a difference.

Look around you, note carefully what you see, and take bearings on landmarks or put a stick in the ground. This is home base. But even though it's home, take your pack with you when you leave to go exploring. Imagine how stupid you'd feel if you left your pack behind and couldn't find it again. From now on, everyone stays tightly together. You don't want to risk becoming separated. First, head for high ground, or climb a tree for a better view. Follow a compass course out from home base so you can find your way back. Nothing? OK, back to home base.

Next, start making short, straight-line reconnaissance runs out and back to all the cardinal and intercardinal points. If that turns up nothing, then it's time to start a search pattern.

Take out pencil and paper. From home base, head in any cardinal direction (write it down). Walk for a mile, or about thirty minutes (write that down, too). Stop, turn 90 degrees and begin walking one-mile legs (and recording all this, along with landmarks passed) until you make a complete square that brings you back to home base. You will have covered a square mile. If you find nothing,

make more one-mile squares by heading out in the remaining three cardinal directions to give you a thoroughly covered four square miles. In an area as large as that, you're bound to find something you can identify positively on your map.

A word of caution, though: Forget about any of these scouting activities if dusk is descending. Being lost in the dark is about as bad as it gets. Until, that is, a storm hits as well. So pitch camp, get settled, make a fire, and start organizing a plan of action for tomorrow. Consider how you will find your way out, or how you can help others find their way in to you.

This last option, the one of staying put and signaling for help, may become a realistic one if you simply can't get a grip on the situation. You can help searchers by staying out in the open or on high ground. You can build a smoky fire (don't burn the forest down in the process) and make noise with a whistle. Yelling doesn't carry far and ruins your voice so you can't properly thank your rescuers. And you can lay out distress signals on the ground. Don't move about. Stay in one place and let them know where it is. Make yourself conspicuous, even if it means wearing plaids and stripes together. With any luck, it won't come to that.

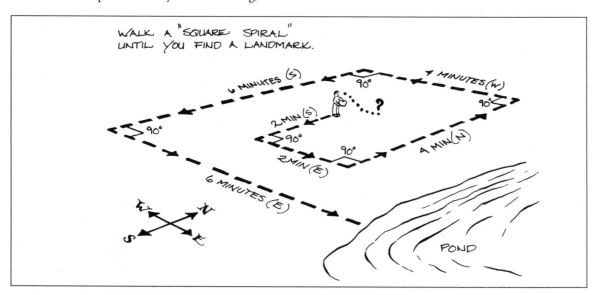

Chapter Six

LOOKING TO NATURE FOR CLUES

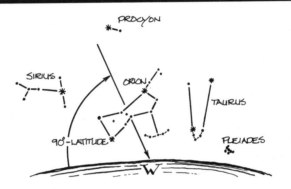

When looking to nature for clues about direction, look to the sky first. What you'll find at ground level isn't going to help nearly as much or as consistently.

Most of what we hear about "nature's guideposts" is either misleading or just plain wrong. The best example is that old saying about moss growing on the north side of trees in the Northern Hemisphere. Go for a walk in the Pacific Northwest, or in any dense, damp forest. You'll see moss on the north, all right. And some on the south, some on the north *and* south, and some on all sides. The "logic" behind this bit of folklore is that the north side gets less (or no) sunlight, so the moss flourishes. In reality, what is more important to moss or lichens is moist surroundings, which can be affected by the wind as well as the sun. Therefore the prevailing winds, local weather, and even the surrounding landscape can determine where you'll find moss.

Here are some other well-known bits of wayfinding lore to be wary of:

Now we return to camp. While eating supper we very naturally speak of better fare, as musty bread and spoiled bacon are not palatable. Soon I see Hawkins down by the boat, taking up the sextant—rather a strange proceeding for him—and I question him concerning it. He replies that he is trying to find the latitude and longitude of the nearest pie.

—The Exploration of the Colorado
River and Its Canyons
John Wesley Powell
Dover Publications, 1961

Snow in the Northern Hemisphere tends to be finer and less granular on the north side of a hill, mountain, or ridge. (In practice such distinctions are fuzzy at best, and often overwhelmed by effects of local terrain and microclimate.)

Snow will melt slower on north-facing slopes in the northern hemisphere. (This one is often true.)

The branches of most trees in the world's temperate regions grow better and are bushier on the side facing the noon sun—although common spruce, firs, and cedars are not affected in this way. (There are too many other factors at work for this to be reliable.)

Almost all trees that stand in the open have thicker annual rings on their north sides (Northern Hemisphere) with the heart of the tree closest to the south. (Growth rings are completely unreliable, since variable width is the normal response to innumerable stress factors.)

Southern slopes have more and thicker vegetation than northern slopes. (Possibly true for steep slopes in extreme high-latitude climates.)

Anthills north of the equator are on the south side of objects. (Unverified, to the best of my knowledge.)

Sunflowers are supposed to face the noon sun. (Observations suggest they more often face the rising sun, and besides, how often are sunflowers at hand?)

Paint fades and peels first on the side that gets the most sun. (Strong prevailing winds from another direction would put the lie to this, and if you're looking at a house, you're probably not lost.)

Similarly, all over the world there are specific plants that are reputed to be able to point out directions. Here in the U.S., from Ohio to the Rockies and Texas to Minnesota, you can find the pilot weed (*Silphium lacinatum*). It grows to about four feet and mostly holds its leaves in a north-south alignment when it's in sunlight. Often called the compass of the prairies, it gets honorable mention in Longfellow's "Evangeline."

"Look at this vigorous plant that lifts its head from the meadow,

There are many ways to navigate with-
out a map or compass, but I habitually
use only two, the sun and the wind,
and then only as backups. Knowing
where they should be in relation to my
route means I am quick to notice if
they shift. If I've veered off my intended
line of travel—easy to do in featureless
terrain like rolling grasslands or contin-
uous forest—I stop and check my loca-
tion. I also check that the wind itself
hasn't shifted, and what the time is so
that I know where the sun should be.

—The Backpacker's Handbook
Chris Townsend
Ragged Mountain Press, 1993

"See how its leaves are turned to the north, as true as the magnet;. . . ."

He's right, but old Henry was obviously no navigator. All of nature's direction-pointing is done in relation to geographic, not magnetic, north.

Another well-known plant, one that grows in the American Southwest and Central Americas, is the giant barrel cactus (*Ferocactus acanthodes*). It grows faster on the shady side than on the sunny side, which almost always makes it lean toward the south. And there are others. File them away as part of your "awareness quotient," much as you're aware that game trails often lead to water, or that swales showing signs of carrying water during storms should lead to brooks, and these should lead to feeder streams, and these should lead ulti-mately to the stream or river that drains the local watershed. Careful reading of the topo map will tell you roughly where the watershed limits are.

It doesn't hurt a bit to know that gulls and other shorebirds seen winging overhead at dusk are probably returning to rookeries on the shore or a nearshore island, or to know how, locally, the vegetation changes with elevation. (The Southwest sequence of saguaro and mesquite yielding to juniper and pinyon, then to oak and ponderosa pine, then to Douglas fir and aspen, and finally to spruce and fir with increasing altitude is a dra-matic example.) Such knowledge brings its own reward of connectedness to the landscape around you. But use such indicators only as rough guides, looking for confirmation from other sources whenever you can. Signs in the heavens are always dependable. So look up.

In this chapter we'll work with the five easiest stars to find. In the Northern Hemisphere there's Polaris; in the Southern Hemisphere we'll use the Southern Cross. East and west will be found with the help of Orion in the winter and Scorpio in the summer. That will take care of your nighttime navigation, which should, for the sake of safety, be limited until you've built up experience.

At daylight you'll have a fifth star to work with: the sun. And, as you'll see, a lot of information can be deduced from it during the course of a day. If you can approximate its path, you have a per-fect reference line from dawn to dusk.

When the stars are your only source of direc-tion, chose your routes carefully and look for other signs along the way.

Finding North and South at Noon

Halfway through its daily journey from sunrise to sunset, the sun is directly to your south (or north in the Southern Hemisphere). This may not be true in the tropics, between latitudes 23½ degrees north and 23½ degrees south. There, the sun is almost directly overhead. And it may not be true in the polar regions, where the sun doesn't set or doesn't rise for months at a time. Everywhere else, though, the sun provides a good indicator of north and south.

The trick is knowing when the sun has reached its halfway point, or noon. The "sun's noon," when shadows run north and south, rarely coincides with the noon on your watch. "Watch noon" is affected by things such as daylight saving time and where you are within your time zone, a band of longitude 15 degrees wide in which every time-piece is set to a common noon. This is done to reduce chaos, because for every degree of longitude you travel east, sun noon occurs four minutes earlier.

Without time zones, someone to the west of center would take their noon lunch break later than someone to the east of center. Then too, the earth's slightly irregular rotation causes watch time, or average time, to differ from the sun's time by as much as 16 minutes. So you might as well forget about using your watch to time the sun's noon.

What you can do instead is use your watch to measure the length of day from sunup to sundown, and then divide that in half to find midday, the sun's noon. Using 24-hour notation, record the time of sunrise and sunset, subtract sunrise from sunset to get the length of day, divide this by two, and add that to the time of sunrise to get noon.

For example, let's say today the upper rim of the sun came into view at 0720 and disappeared below the horizon again at 1738. Subtracting 0720 from 1738 gives 1018. That's the length of time the sun spent above the horizon. Dividing that by two gives 0509, half a day. You then add 0509 to 0720 to get 1229, your local noon.

You now know that at 1229 the sun will throw a shadow that runs north and south (that's geographic, not magnetic, north). This system will work as long as your watch keeps steady time. It even works if your watch is set for another time zone. As long as the period between sunrise and set is measured accurately, you'll be fine.

One drawback to this system is that if you time sunrise first and then sunset, noon has already passed. Luckily though, the sun changes its course through the heavens so slowly that you don't need to take the time of sunrise and sunset on the same day. You could record sunset as you make camp and then sunrise the next morning at breakfast. This way you'll know when to expect noon later that day to check your north/south bearing at lunch.

Of course, where the horizon is obscured by the terrain, you won't be able to time the sunrise or sunset accurately. You'd do well to note these times from the daily almanac of a local newspaper before you head off onto the trail.

This same system will work equally well with a full moon. If the full moon is bright enough to throw a shadow, you have a good north/south indicator around "lunar midnight," when the moon is halfway across the sky. Further, if you know the local sun's noon is at 1230, then you also know the full moon will bear due south at 30 minutes past midnight. This is so because, by definition, the full moon is exactly on the opposite side of the earth from the sun. Warning: It's tough to tell a "full" moon within four days unless you know the date from a calendar or almanac.

North and South from a Shadow

What if your watch has stopped? There is a way of finding where the sun's noon shadow will lie when you have only a rough idea when midday will occur.

The sun travels a uniform arc through the sky, with noon as its midpoint. Whatever its height is at a given time before noon, it will be at an equal height the same length of time after noon. The sun's height is reflected in the shadows it casts. The longest shadows are formed at sunrise and sunset, the shortest at noon. A morning shadow will slowly shorten as midday approaches, and then begin to lengthen as noon passes. If you were to measure that shadow's length in the morning, it would eventually return to the same length sometime in the afternoon. When it did, the sun would have traveled an equal distance each side of noon. Which is how we will find the midday shadow and, from that, north and south.

To do this you'll need a vertical object. A flagpole, ski pole, walking stick, or even a pencil will do, although shadows from taller objects are easier to measure. By some means or other (most likely with a weight dangling from a string), you must be sure the object is plumbed absolutely vertical on a patch of smooth, horizontal ground. Make your first measurement with a piece of string or a stick, and mark the end of the shadow with a stone. Do this when you are sure it is before the sun's noon, yet as close to it as possible (so you won't have long to wait for the next measurement).

Now sit back and watch as the shadow gets smaller and then longer again, all the while changing its direction. Once it has returned to its original length, mark the shadow's end. Connect the two marks with a straight line, and find its middle. That's where the shadow was at noon. A line running from the vertical object to the midpoint of the connecting line will run north and south.

This system works almost everywhere, regardless of your latitude or the time of year. Its only drawbacks are that you have to wait what could be hours during the middle of the day. Then, too, at certain times of the year near the polar circles, the sun's shadows will be so long as to be impractical to measure. And in areas near the equator, shadows are often impractically short, or else they change imperceptibly, making them difficult to measure. But almost everywhere else this is a reliable way to find north and south.

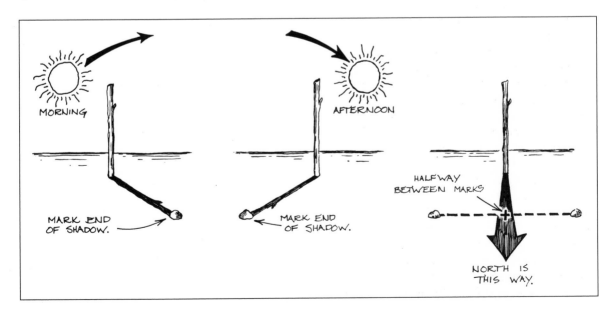

MORNING

MARK END OF SHADOW.

AFTERNOON

MARK END OF SHADOW.

HALFWAY BETWEEN MARKS

NORTH IS THIS WAY.

Quick but Not Accurate

We love things that are quick and simple, ideas or gadgets that get a job done with a minimum of fuss. Sometimes we love their convenience so much that we're willing to overlook how poorly they actually work. So it is with the following.

All three have been an accepted part of wayfinding lore for a long time. They work, but only under the rarest and best of circumstances. The rest of the time they offer only a crude approximation of direction. Try them yourself, checking the results against a compass (adjusted for declination).

South from a Watch

Point the hour hand of your watch at the sun, or line up the hour hand with a shadow from a vertical object. True south (true north in the Southern Hemisphere) should lie halfway between the hour hand and the number 12. (You would want to use the *larger* of the two arcs between the hour hand and 12 for measurements before 6 A.M. or after 6 P.M. but in those hours you'd do as well or better to get a sunrise or sunset bearing, as we'll learn shortly.) If you have a digital watch, draw a clock's face in the dirt to represent an analog watch with the hour hand aimed as described.

Often ignored when explaining this technique is the need to correct for your longitude within the time zone, described earlier in this chapter, and for daylight saving time. But the biggest problem with this system is that the sun's bearing does not change at a constant rate, as does the clock's hour hand, throughout the day. The sun's apparent path through the sky varies with the season and latitude of the observer. While at times the results can be quite close, summer in the middle latitudes of the U.S. brings an average error of 20 degrees. It works best closer to the poles and is almost useless in the tropics.

Following a Shadow

Place in the ground so that it is vertical a straight stick at least three feet long. Mark the end of its shadow. Wait at least 15 minutes until the end of the shadow has moved, and mark the new position. A line connecting the marks should run east and west, with your first mark being westernmost.

Unlike the watch/sun system, this one can get you reasonably close to an accurate direction. The principle is that as the sun moves westward its shadow moves eastward. But the sun's motion also has a northern component as it gains height in the morning and a southern one as it loses altitude in the afternoon, which can throw off your line. The sun is closest to moving directly westward around sun noon (not watch noon). Done within two hours of sun noon, you can get a direction that is accurate to within 10 degrees. The method is not reliable in the early morning or late afternoon, but is accurate all day long during the time of the equinoxes (March 21 and September 23).

Noon from a Shadow

You should be able to tell when it is noon because shadows are at their shortest then.

Technically this is true. But the change in lengths around midday is so slight compared with changes in the sun's bearing, which are quite rapid, that it would be almost impossible to say exactly when noon occurs. It is this same fact that makes noon the best time for finding an east/west line by shadows as described above.

Movements of Sunrise and Sunset

The sun doesn't always rise in the east and set in the west. In fact, it does this only twice a year—at the equinoxes, when the sun is over the equator, around March 21 and September 23.

The rest of the year, the sun rises and sets north or south of east and west. For example, if you were just south of the Arctic Circle there would be days when the sun rose far north of east, headed southward, and then returned to set far north of west. On those same days, someone on the equator would see the sun rise almost due east, pass almost overhead, and then set almost due west.

For most of us, the sun rises within a range of 30 degrees north or south of geographic east, giving a very rough, but useful, indication of direction. The sun's exact bearings depend on the time of year and your latitude (how far north or south of the equator you are).

In the Northern Hemisphere, after the fall equinox in late September, the sun rises farther to the south of east each day. It reaches its southernmost limit during the winter solstice, December 21. By the spring equinox, in late March, the sun is rising directly in the east. From then on, it begins to rise farther to the north of east as each

day passes, reaching its northernmost limit at the summer solstice on June 21. It then heads back toward the equator, rising ever closer to geographic east until, on September 23, the fall equinox, it comes up exactly in the east and sets exactly in the west.

You can use this cycle to give you a highly visible line of reference. While still in familiar surroundings, watch the sun for a few days, noting its position in the sky at different times. Get an idea of its bearings when it's rising and setting, and its height at midday. This pattern will soon become part of your directional sense, sending a warning when you stray in the wrong direction.

How Long until Sunset?

Hold up your hand at arm's length and measure how many "fingers" the sun is above your visible horizon. Each horizontal "finger" equals about 15 minutes before sunset. Therefore, four fingers equal about an hour. Using your other hand as well, eight fingers represent two hours—which is the limit of this trick unless you have an excess of digits.

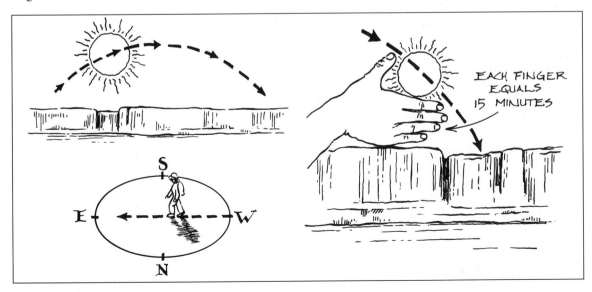

EACH FINGER EQUALS 15 MINUTES

Bearings from Sunrise and Sunset

You can use the sun's rising and setting to get accurate bearings. Besides being helpful on their own, they can be used to determine local declination by showing the difference between the sun's magnetic bearing (from the compass) and its geographic bearing as it comes up over the horizon. And don't worry if there isn't a clear horizon or you miss sunrise by a few minutes. At this time of day, the sun's bearing changes very slowly, about one degree every eight minutes in Florida and every four minutes in northern Canada. So it can come up behind low hills or you can sleep a few minutes late, and you'll still get a reasonably accurate bearing.

Another handy bit of information is that the amount the sun varies north or south of east upon rising is the same amount it varies from west when setting. If you know one, you know the other.

You can find the bearings of sunrise and sunset by using the circular chart on the opposite page, which was adapted from one published by David Burch, a master navigator, in his excellent book *Emergency Navigation: Pathfinding Techniques for the Inquisitive and Prudent Mariner* (International Marine, 1986, 1990). There's a blank version you can photocopy for your own calculations in the Appendix. The chart gives the sun's amplitude, or number of degrees north or south of 0 degrees (which represents due east or west). This is not the sun's bearing. To get that, you have to do some addition or subtraction. Just follow the step-by-step procedure and you'll see how it's done.

Working Out the Bearings

1: Look up the sun's maximum amplitude (the farthest it travels north or south of 0 degrees during the year) at your latitude. An approximate latitude will do fine. We'll use 47 degrees north, about right for Fargo, North Dakota, where the sun has a maximum amplitude of 36 degrees.

2: Scale the north/south baseline of the circular chart for 36 degrees on each side of the 0-

degree mark. This can be done by halving: Halfway between 0 degrees and the circumference (which represents 36 degrees) is 18 degrees. Mark that. Halfway between 0 degrees and 18 degrees is 9 degrees. Mark that. Keep dividing each space on the baseline by half until you run out of room, or get bored.

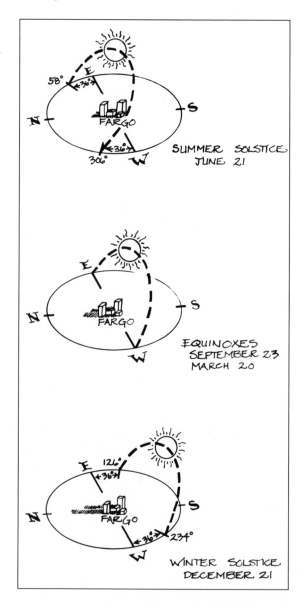

SUMMER SOLSTICE
JUNE 21

EQUINOXES
SEPTEMBER 23
MARCH 20

WINTER SOLSTICE
DECEMBER 21

3: Find today's date along the circumference. Let's say it's August 1. Draw a line from the date toward, and perpendicular to, the baseline. Where the lines intersect is the sun's amplitude for that day on that latitude. In this case, it's 27 degrees to the north of 0 degrees.

4: To find the sun's bearing when it rises, subtract north amplitude, or add south amplitude, to 90 degrees (east). In our case, we subtract 27 degrees from 90 degrees to get 63 degrees. When the sun rises it will bear 063 degrees.

5: To find the sun's bearing when it sets, add north amplitude, or subtract south amplitude, from 270 degrees (west). In our case we add 27 degrees to 270 degrees to get 297 degrees. When the sun sets it will bear 297 degrees.

No one is expected to bring this chart along for use in an emergency. This is something you do before heading out, so you have the sun's bearings when and if you need them. The bearings won't change much during the course of a week, or within a few hundred miles north or south of where they were taken.

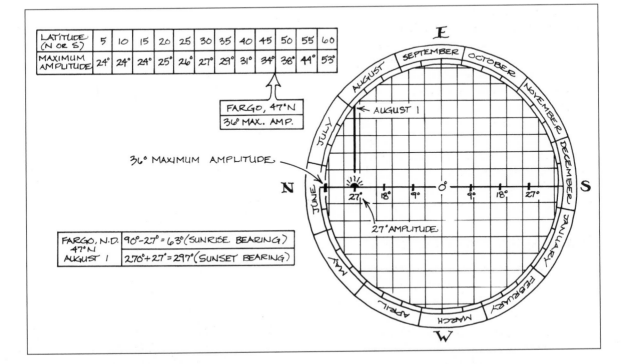

LATITUDE (N or S)	5	10	15	20	25	30	35	40	45	50	55	60
MAXIMUM AMPLITUDE	24°	24°	24°	25°	26°	27°	29°	31°	34°	38°	44°	53°

FARGO, 47°N
36° MAX. AMP.

36° MAXIMUM AMPLITUDE

FARGO, N.D. 47°N AUGUST 1	90°-27° = 63° (SUNRISE BEARING)
	270°+27° = 297° (SUNSET BEARING)

27° AMPLITUDE

E
N
S
W

135

Polaris

Hiking at night is not advisable for beginners, except around the time of full moon when you are crossing clear, open ground. (With experience, you'll find that hiking trails at night isn't a problem, especially if you carry a good headlamp or flashlight.) It can be useful to get bearings from the night sky, however—bearings you can use the next day. To make sense of the night sky, you'll do well to forget modern science and see the stars as folks did before Copernicus. Think of the heavens as the inside of a black bowl (the Polynesians saw it as a half-shell) with a fixed pattern of stars painted on it. While the Earth stays still, this celestial bowl rotates around us once a day using a line through the geographic north and south poles as its axis, with each star circling over us at a fixed latitude.

The handiest of all stars is Polaris, sitting almost at the bowl's axis directly over the north pole. This is a wonderful coincidence of nature, giving us a constant point of reference that never seems to move. Actually it is not precisely over the pole, but rotates in a very small counterclockwise orbit around it, but the discrepancy is too small to be noticed by the naked eye and makes no difference for our purposes. In the tropics, Polaris begins to fall too close to the horizon for clarity. It becomes hard to spot south of 10 degrees north latitude, and disappears completely near the equator.

Another wonderful coincidence is that constellations rotating around Polaris can be used as pointers to help find it. This is helpful, because Polaris is not a particularly bright star and doesn't stand out much in a crowd.

The best indicators are the two "Dippers." Polaris is the last star in the handle of the Little Dipper, which is not the easiest constellation to find. But the Big Dipper is one of the most prominent constellations in the sky, and the stars that make up the outer side of the Big Dipper's cup act as pointers to Polaris. If you line up the star Dubhe, at the cup's outer lip, with the star Merak, inside the cup, they make a straight line that runs right to Polaris. The distance to Polaris along this line is five times that between Dubhe

and Merak. It's sometimes useful to know the relationship between the two Dippers: If water were poured from one, it would be caught in the other, and their handles bend in opposite directions.

If the Big Dipper is not visible, you can use Cassiopeia—a giant "W" or "M" (depending on the time of night) floating in the sky. If you were standing on Polaris, Cassiopeia would always look like an "M." A perpendicular drawn from a line connecting the legs of the M and taken from the trailing leg will hit Polaris at twice the M's width. If you can see the Big Dipper, Cassiopeia is across from it on the opposite side of Polaris. Incidentally, constellations revolve counterclockwise around Polaris.

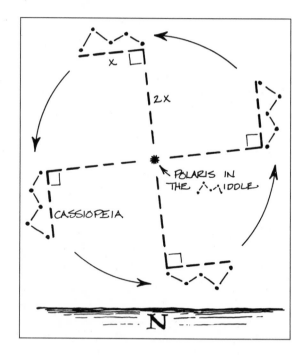

Latitude from Polaris

Polaris's height above an unimpeded horizon (no intervening hills or vegetation) tells us our approximate latitude. Ancient navigators knew the latitudes for all their destinations. They would sail, ride, or walk until Polaris showed that they were on that latitude and then turn east or west toward their goal, keeping Polaris at the same height.

The "height" of the star is measured in degrees, the number of degrees equaling your latitude. Sailors use a sextant to ascertain this, but it's doubtful that you'll want to lug one of those around, although Major John Wesley Powell, John C. Fremont, and other Western explorers used them. Instead you can use your fingers, sacrificing accuracy for convenience. Measure 10 degrees as shown, or hold your arm outstretched in front of you as if giving someone an enthusiastic "thumb's up." The distance from the fleshy part of your hand (beneath the pinky joint) to the tip of your upstretched thumb is about 15 degrees. Now rotate your hand 90 degrees; the vertical distance represented by your thumb's width is 2 to 3 degrees. Rotate your hand again, so your thumb points down. The distance from one knuckle to the next is about 3 degrees. You'll be lucky to get within a degree or two of your latitude, and every degree equals 60 miles, so this technique is of limited utility at best. But exercises like this somehow help us into a proper relationship with the earth and heavens.

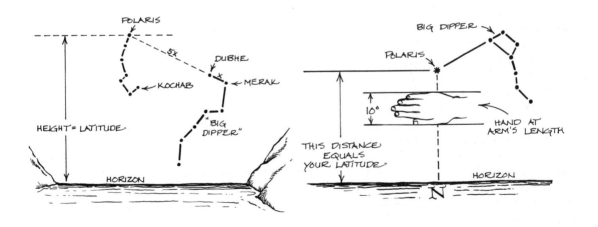

The Southern Cross

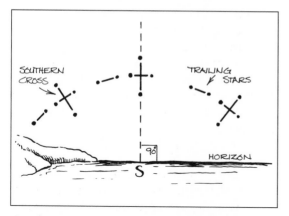

The Southern Cross is visible as far north as 25 degrees of latitude, but only for short periods during the night. Its use as a navigational aid is limited north of the equator because the celestial south pole then lies below the horizon. The only time it is a good indicator of south is when the Cross appears to be vertical.

The farther you head south from the equator, the longer the Southern Cross stays above the horizon, and from 37 degrees south latitude southward, the Cross remains visible throughout the night.

Good news and bad news. First the good news. There's a star in the Southern Hemisphere comparable to Polaris, almost directly over the south pole. It's the star Sigma in the constellation Octans—it has no common name. It will tell you which way is south.

The bad news is that the star is so dim as to be almost impossible to find with the naked eye, and is surrounded by similarly weak stars. But all is not lost. Again, as with Polaris, there are pointers to this star (or at least where this star would be if we could see it), in this case in the constellation of the Southern Cross.

To many who see it for the first time, the Southern Cross is a bit of a letdown. Compared with the northern pointers of Cassiopeia and the Big Dipper, it is small and unobtrusive. To some, its four brightest stars look more like a kite, because there is no star at the point where the two arms of the cross would intersect. There is also a nearby "False Cross," which has five stars.

But the true Cross can be confirmed by two closely spaced, very bright stars that trail behind (stars in the Southern Hemisphere travel clockwise around the pole) the crosspiece. These two stars are often easier to pick out than the Cross itself. Look for them.

The long axis of the Cross points to within three degrees of the celestial south pole—not an exact pointer but very close. The distance is four-and-a-half times the long axis of the cross from its bottom.

The toe of the star-gazer is often stubbed.

—Russian proverb

Other Stars

Observed Motion of Any Star

Here's a way to get directions when identifying individual stars is impossible. It is based on the principle that stars travel from east to west.

Sight on any star in mid-sky (stay away from stars near the poles) and note its position relative to something on the ground (a tree top, peak, or nearby stick you have planted for the purpose). Give the star about 20 minutes and see which way it travels.

If it heads downward, it's in the west. If it goes upward, it's in the east. If it goes to the right, it's in the south. If it goes to the left, it's in the north.

Orion

Highly visible in the winter sky (or summer sky in the Southern Hemisphere), Orion circles the earth on the celestial equator. The leading and north-ernmost star in its belt is actually on the equator, and therefore rises in the east and sets in the west no matter what latitude you see it from.

Since you may not remember which is the correct star, or be able to pick out the one that is leading or northernmost, use the middle star—the belt's "buckle"—which is only one degree from the equator.

It is easier to find west with Orion than it is to find east. Wait until the constellation begins to set and then see where the "buckle" touches the horizon. In order to find east, you have to know what the constellation looks like emerging from below the horizon or, once up, how to retrace the buckle's path back to where it popped up. Both are hard to do.

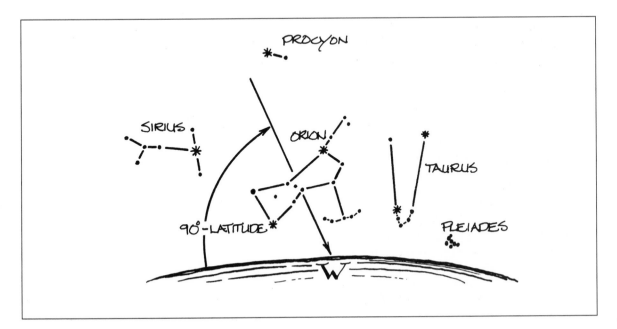

Chapter Seven

EXTREME ENVIRONMENTS

Mountains

Regardless of where you are, you'll be able to use and adapt the information in the preceding chapters. So-called extreme environments may be comparatively easy to navigate even if they are hard to traverse. Mountains are just such a place.

If anything, navigating in mountains is somewhat easier than on level terrain, because of the numerous visible landmarks, most notably mountain peaks. Even when conditions are unfavorable it is often harder to get lost in mountains. In order to get disoriented, you usually have to climb out of one river drainage and into another—more often than not a hard-to-miss transition.

Of course there are some adjustments to make when you take your navigating skills to the vertical world of mountains and steep hill-country. Distances taken directly from a map are misleading because they read as if the landscape had been flattened. One "map" mile between two points could very well turn out to be nearer two "real-world" miles over steep terrain. To better understand this, review the sections of Chapter 2 on Distance, Slope Profiles, and Slope Gradients.

If the contour lines on your topo map leave you in any doubt, or you have only a planimetric map (without contour lines), one sure sign of steeply rising land is a trail with a series of switchbacks or hairpin turns on your map—the only route a trail can take to avoid a hard direct climb. But most often, maps will not be so obvious in their clues. Unless you are used to map reading in alpine areas, you'll be astounded at how much bigger and steeper things actually are. You may be good at interpreting contour lines, but there is little in most people's experience to help make the transition from hills to mountains.

Compasses are also better suited to level going. Try this for yourself: Take a bearing from your backyard of your neighbor's chimney. It doesn't take much of an upward angle to bind up the needle until it is no longer free to swing. In practice, though, this really isn't a problem. If you're close enough to a cliff, peak, or other landmark to have to crane your neck upward for a bearing, you probably don't need the bearing to navigate. If you

do, simply take a bearing off the base of the landmark; it will be accurate enough.

In general, you'll have less need for constant reference to your compass in the mountains than on level ground, because of the prominent landmarks. In fact, you'll seldom keep actual "courses." You'll generally be heading somewhere specific, such as a pass or peak, and leaving from a natural feature such as a riverside meadow or a canyon-bottom trailhead. The trail or unmarked route will simply follow the line of least resistance while you read the lie of the land. The path up a steep slope will often turn in switchbacks to reduce the grade—so you are continually changing directions and at no time heading directly toward your goal. When you can't keep your destination in sight, you may find it helpful to use intermediate landmarks.

Upon reaching a summit, you'll typically be able to orient yourself by comparing the surrounding high points with peaks shown on your map. Use compass bearings as necessary to put things into perspective. Use elevation information to help. If the map shows your elevation, compare that with peaks above or below your horizontal line of sight. Use the tree line or snow line to help gauge the height of other mountains. In areas where the vegetation changes predictably and dramatically with elevation, you can use these clues to estimate the heights of various landmarks. If you are confused during the climb, don't worry—as you gain height, landmarks become fewer, more obvious, and more easily identified.

Once you have arrived at the summit, make careful plans for your descent. It is much easier to get disoriented going down toward the rest of the world than going up to a small point in the sky. Take advantage of the spectacular view around you to pick out your route. Look for landmarks, turning points, or big clues that indicate you are off course. Think about aiming off, and identify naturally occurring brackets. It would be good to make notes on the map to which you can refer as you descend, but few people do this. In stormy weather or dense clouds, just the conditions when route finding is difficult, making notes is impossible. It would be better to work out compass bearings in advance and have them handy to refer to when required.

Altimeters and GPS Receivers

Sometimes it's difficult to take bearings of or from a shrouded summit. Wouldn't it be nice if there were some other instrument to help mountaineers find their way? Actually, there are two.

The *altimeter* is nothing more than a portable barometer, an instrument that measures air pressure. The principle is that as you go up, air pressure (the weight of the air) decreases at a uniform rate. As you descend, it increases. So if you calibrate a barometer to read these changes in pressure as feet (or meters) you can always tell your elevation. And that's a good thing to know.

If you're sure you're at 1,800 feet, then you must be somewhere along the 1,800-foot contour line—which eliminates a lot of real estate. That contour line provides an excellent line of position that can be crossed with a bearing or a natural feature (such as a trail, ridge, stream, or notch) to give you a fix. Unfortunately, uncontrollable factors can throw off an altimeter's readings. These are changes in temperature and variations in air pressure caused by weather.

The heart of an altimeter is a metal capsule that encloses a partial vacuum. The surrounding air pressure forces the capsule to expand and contract, and this movement is connected either to a pointer that moves along a scale or to a digital readout. But the capsule will also flex under changes of temperature, thereby causing false readings.

The best defense is to prevent temperature variations. Carry your altimeter in an outside pack pocket, rather than in a shirt pocket, so it stays at the same temperature as the ambient air. And don't expect an altimeter adjusted in a warm cabin to be accurate out on the glacier. Temperature problems can be pretty much eliminated by using a temperature-compensated altimeter, but the convenience and precision will cost you more—around $200 in 1995.

Then there is weather, which no one can do anything about. It's possible to go to sleep with the altimeter displaying one height and to wake up in the morning to have it read a significantly different one. Your tent didn't levitate. All it takes is a shift in the barometric pressure to make you think the altimeter (or you) has gone nuts. This can be even more puzzling when you are underway. You won't be able to differentiate between the effects of the changing altitude and meteorological changes, making a complete guessing game of your elevation.

The best way to get accurate readings is to adjust the altimeter every chance you get. Each time you come to, or are about to leave from, a position that has its elevation noted on the map, check the altimeter. Reset if necessary. To minimize the effect of weather changes, try to make these adjustments at least once an hour.

Whether altimeters are worth the effort or expense is up to you. Some climbers swear by them. Others—probably the majority—swear *at* them.

For not much more than a good altimeter, you can buy a Global Positioning System (GPS) receiver, which will fix your position *and* your altitude and can be used in fog, darkness, or your tent. See the Appendix for more information.

Snow

Snow changes things, filling in the landscape like spackle on cheap wallboard. Areas exposed to wind-blown snow develop new and ever-changing contours. Depressions are leveled out, drifts fill ravines, turning them into flats, and ground characteristics such as rocks and vegetation are covered. Trails disappear, blazes and signs are hidden, and bodies of water look like open fields. Some of the subtle indicators you depend on during the warmer months are gone—but the principal landmarks and the principles of magnetic navigation remain.

An all-white environment reduces depth perception and judgment of distances, and this is made worse by the low contrast of weak light from gray winter skies, or the snow blindness caused by dazzling sun. In general, though, snow poses more problems to travel than to navigation.

You will encounter three main types of terrain in snow, each posing its own navigational problems.

The first is rolling wooded lowlands or foothills on the fringe of a mountain range. This terrain provides little in the way of direction-finding clues. Slopes may be exaggerated or softened by drifting snow, so that in some areas the contour lines can deceive as much as they inform. In this case, look to the more up-to-date portrayal of back roads that you'll usually find on the planimetric maps distributed by the U.S. Forest Service, Land Management Bureau, or local parks. Knowing where these roads are, and where they lead to, can be a godsend. Of course, when handling any type of map, remember that all that cold white stuff is only water in disguise. Get it on a map warmed from your pocket and you have a map that won't last too much longer. The solution is to use a transparent, waterproof map case or to treat your map with one of the waterproofing compounds available for the purpose. Alternatively, if available for the region you're visiting, use a map printed on waterproof plastic such as those from Trails Illustrated (see the Appendix).

Trail-marking cairns are likely to be blanketed, and when snow is on the trees, blazes may be hidden as well. In general, only the higher and more obvious landmarks will be visible, and these may be rare in this terrain. One of the few remaining natural references is a fast-flowing river or stream that rarely freezes over. These can make good lines of position or baselines, but following them can be hazardous. Sections can be covered by snow that collapses if you inadvertently venture onto it. Also, streams always take the quickest way downhill and can lead you to steep, dangerous slopes. Large frozen lakes and rivers are also good position indicators and can be excellent "highways" upon which to travel and make good time, though you must be extremely wary of thin ice. Navigating on large lakes can be very difficult, however, when you can't see either shore due to a white-out or blizzard. And snow-covered lakes are not always flat, because the wind can create large drifts.

The second frequently encountered terrain is the subalpine area below the tree line, where your best guides and routes to follow will be along the valleys, canyons, and ravines that have not been filled in. Knowing the direction in which a valley runs may be enough to keep you from getting lost (as long as you really are in the valley you *think* you're in). Do this by keeping constant track of your route. And do not depend on the prevailing winds as a reference in this type of landscape. They will be twisted by the land, coming at you from all directions each time you turn a corner.

The third area of travel in snow country is the high alpine zone above the tree line—the domain of the mountaineer and the ski tourer. Here your greatest enemy will be the snow in the air as well as that on the ground. Know where you are at all times, because visibility can deteriorate quite suddenly. At the first sign of an approaching snowstorm, or when dense clouds start to form, pinpoint your position with bearings on a map. As the weather closes in, look for large dark shadows in the misty whiteout to use as intermediate landmarks along the way. A heavy snowfall can obscure all clues rapidly. There is also the danger of your suffering from vertigo in a world where there is no clear demarcation between sky and ground. At times it can be difficult to know whether you are moving up or down. One useful trick is to throw a snowball ahead of you. If it appears to stick in mid-air, the ground ahead must slope upward. If it lands lower than your feet you are on a downward slope and need to proceed very carefully. If it disappears from view, back off quickly; you could be on a cornice or the edge of a steep drop.

Thankfully, whiteouts are not that common, but they are certainly treacherous when you're traveling near crevasses. Plan escape routes in case of bad weather, or be equipped and prepared to camp or snowhole until the weather clears. Even if you could travel a reliable compass course, don't do it. You could walk straight into a crevasse. In a pinch, you might be able to retrace your tracks if the wind has not obliterated them, but this can be tedious and dangerous if you can only see a few feet ahead. You may also wind up following someone else's tracks.

When the weather is good, dead-reckoning techniques work well even on glaciers or other open snowfields, *most* of the time. But for intricate routes on crevassed glaciers lacking reliable landmarks, you will need greater navigation precision than dead reckoning can provide, which means you will have to make your own guides. All the information found in Chapter 3 about how to follow a straight course when there are no landmarks applies here. Look it over now. You can use back bearings, or even other members of your party. But one of the best ways is to make your own transit markers using wands you've carried along for the purpose.

These wands are often made of lightweight split-bamboo poles with strips of cloth tied to them. You can make them yourself from green bamboo sticks sold as plant supports at garden supply stores. Slit the top for a few inches, slide in any brightly colored, durable material, tie it in place, and then tape the top of the wand shut. Make everything strong. Wands should be 36 to 48 inches long. If you need wands at all, chances are you'll need a lot of them.

Wands can be used as transits to help you keep a straight course, or as trail markers for your return trip. When used as the latter, make sure you space them closely enough that the next marker comes into view as the last member of your party passes the previous one. Under no circumstances should the last person leave a wand before the new one has been positively sighted. Then, and only then, is that previous wand collected for later use, and so as not to leave a maze of old and potentially confusing trails. Tilt wands to point toward the next one along. Don't place them in hollows or on the downside of ridges where they will be hard to see on the way back. Mark important wands, those that indicate course changes or dangers, differently. The standard sign for a crevasse or danger is two crossed wands.

Finally, ski tourers and mountaineers need to know how to recognize potential avalanche danger both on the map and on the ground. Avalanches usually occur on slopes of 25 to 45 degrees. If in doubt, stay off steep slopes. Ridges are safer, as are wide valley bottoms. Watch for avalanche chutes such as tree-free corridors on forested mountain sides, and don't camp below these! Snow travelers should study this subject well (there are several good books on the subject), and know how to dig test pits and what to do if an avalanche occurs.

Now for a change of pace, here's a little quiz. Which of the following four pieces of folklore are true?

- Snow tends to be finer and less granular on the north side of ridges, trees, and other prominent features.
- In winter, poplar trees are darker on their north sides.
- Solitary coniferous trees are bushiest on their south sides.
- North slopes are less densely packed with snow, but are icier.

Well? How did you do? Here's the answer: Trust none of the above.

Take all the precautions you can when traveling in snow. Those gentle flakes can be killers when they gang up on you.

Deserts

The deserts of the American Southwest are one of the toughest environments in which to navigate— *much* harder than mountains, for example— mostly due to the presence of canyons and arroyos (deep washes), which tend to obstruct your path quite suddenly. Since they cut into the topography, rather than rising above it, the flat, open plain or tableland you thought to cross can stop you cold with little advance warning. Often you'll have to plot avoidance bearings for unseen canyons, then skirt them via compass bearings as discussed in Chapter 4.

The popular image of deserts paints them as vast, open spaces, but many, such as the Colorado Plateau, are extremely convoluted in their topography. We think of deserts as fields of sand dunes, yet sand dunes are a novelty in America's deserts. We think of deserts as flat, yet the canyonlands of the Southwest have more vertical terrain than most mountain ranges. And we tend to think of deserts as barren, yet some, such as the Sonoran, are anything but that. In the flat Sonoran terrain, obscuring vegetation such as mesquite and palo verde trees make sighting on distant landmarks difficult.

Nevertheless, bearings on distant landmarks are the staple of desert navigation. Often there is a lack of notable features in the foreground, but a circle of larger (and often quite striking) landmarks in the far distance.

Be cautious before taking those first steps from the trailhead or base camp. Distances in the clear, dry air are deceptive. Mountains that appear to be only a few miles off may in actuality be 20 or 30 miles away, and distances across wide valleys are even harder to judge. Your goal could be in view yet still take many days to reach. An oft-quoted rule of thumb for desert travel is to multiply your estimated distance by a factor of three to compensate for natural underestimation.

Once out there, look to those bold, distant features, using bearings from your compass and information from good (recently updated) topo maps. One of the more confusing aspects of desert travel is the maze-like network of backroads pass-

The canyon country does not always inspire love. To many it appears barren, hostile, repellent—a fearsome land of rock and heat, sand dunes and quicksand, cactus, thornbush, scorpion, rattlesnake, and agoraphobic distances. To those who see our land in that manner, the best reply is, yes, you are right, it is a dangerous and terrible place. Enter at your own risk. Carry water. Avoid the noonday sun. Try to ignore the vultures. Pray frequently.

—The Journey Home
Edward Abbey
Dutton, 1977

ing through it. The less substantial ones get blown away or washed out, and many that seem quite good are not included on the map. Checking with local land-management agents or rangers before using a map is a good way to find out the current status of these constantly changing roads. When following a road, keep meticulous track of each turnoff, fork, junction, direction turned, and mileage covered. Since there are rarely any road signs in the desert, this is the only way to know where you are. And that's important, because one wrong turn can lead into a bewildering network of backroads from which there seems no way out.

In the desert, as in any extreme environment, caution and preparation are the keys to finding your way.

APPENDIX

Bearings of Sunrise and Sunset

1: Find the sun's maximum amplitude for your latitude.
2: Scale the north/south baseline of the circular chart for the maximum amplitude on each side of the 0-degree mark.
3: Find today's date along the circumference. Draw a line from the date toward, and perpendicular to, the baseline. Where the lines intersect is the sun's amplitude for that day at that latitude.

4: To find the sun's bearing when it rises, in the Northern Hemisphere subtract north amplitude from, or add south amplitude to, 90 degrees (east).
5: To find the sun's bearing when it sets, in the Northern Hemisphere, add north amplitude to, or subtract south amplitude from, 270 degrees (west).

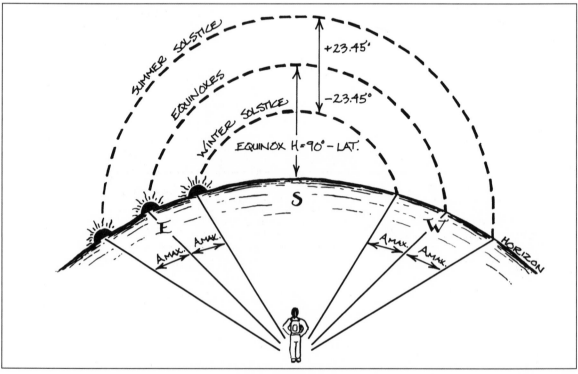

LATITUDE (N OR S)	5	10	15	20	25	30	35	40	45	50	55	60
MAXIMUM AMPLITUDE	24°	24°	24°	25°	26°	27°	29°	31°	34°	38°	44°	53°

NORTH AMPLITUDES	SOUTH AMPLITUDES
SUNRISE BEARING = 90° – AMPLITUDE	SUNRISE BEARING = 90° + AMPLITUDE
SUNSET BEARING = 270° + AMPLITUDE	SUNSET BEARING = 270° – AMPLITUDE

Declination Corrections

In an earlier chapter you learned easy ways to compensate for declination, the angular difference between geographic north and magnetic north. But there may be times when those methods are not available to you, or you may simply prefer the logic of numbers. If so, here is how you can correct for declination:

From map to compass.

To adjust a direction taken from a map to be used with a compass, do the following:

East declination: subtract. For example, if the direction on a map is 90 degrees and the declination is 12 degrees east, the comparable direction on a compass would be 78 degrees.

West declination: add. If the direction on a map is 90 degrees and the declination is 8 degrees west, the comparable direction on a compass would be 98 degrees.

From compass to map.

To adjust a direction taken by a compass to be used on a map, do the following:

East declination: add. If a compass shows a bearing of 90 degrees and the declination is 12 degrees east, the comparable direction on a map would be 102 degrees.

West declination: subtract. If a compass shows a bearing of 90 degrees and the declination is 8 degrees west, the comparable direction on a map would be 82 degrees.

How to Remember These Rules

There's quite a bit here to recall and, to make it worse, the rules all sound very much alike. Luckily, though, you will only need to know the two rules for your particular declination, be it east or west. So keep only those in mind and you'll be OK.

WEST declination: Add from map to compass, subtract from compass to map.

EAST declination: Add from compass to map, subtract from map to compass.

There's also a mnemonic device that has been used by sailors for the past few centuries and has probably kept a lot of ships off the rocks.

Declination EAST, compass least.

Declination WEST, compass best.

What this means is that with an east declination, the map reading is greater (best) and the compass reading smaller (least)—by the amount of declination. With a west declination, the compass reading is best and the map reading least, by the amount of declination. In each case, you simply add or subtract declination.

Here's one last trick to jump-start your memory. Think of the saying . . .

Empty sea, add water.

Empty sea becomes MTC (Map To Compass). Add water becomes add W (west).

MTC, add W.

Thus, when converting a bearing from map to compass, add west declination. (Again—declination west, compass best.) From this you can surmise that you would subtract east declination. (Declination east, compass least.) Or from compass (C) to (T) map (M) you would subtract west and add east.

If you don't want to bother with this, or if you have more important things to remember, write down the rule for declination in your area (east or west) on the map or glue it on the back of your compass.

Incidentally, when you're describing directions, you won't want to go above 360 degrees. If an addition comes to more than 360 degrees, subtract 360 degrees. For example, if you have to add 20 degrees to 355 degrees the answer is 375 degrees—minus 360 degrees, which is 15 degrees.

The same 360-degree rule applies to subtraction. If you have to subtract 25 degrees from 15 degrees, borrow 360 degrees to start with. Add it to the 15 degrees you want to subtract from. Then subtract 25 degrees from 375 degrees, and the answer is 350 degrees.

Metric Conversion Tables

An Act of Congress in 1966 legalized the metric system here in the U.S. Almost every other country has gone metric because it is logical and easier to work with, but the U.S. refuses to change. As a token gesture, USGS topos have a distance scale in kilometers, as well as in miles and yards, and U.S. nautical charts have begun a long-term conversion to metric. Almost all other parts of the world there are only kilometers and meters. So if you're an American resident carrying a passport, it's a safe bet you'd better learn to think metric.

The following conversions might be helpful.

Rough comparisons.

4 inch = 10 centimeter, or 1 inch = 2.5 centimeters

1 foot = .3 meter, or 1 meter = 3¼ feet

39 inches = 1 meter, or 1 yard = 1 meter

⅝ mile = 1 kilometer, or 5 miles = 8 kilometers

Accurate comparisons.

1 millimeter (mm) = .039 inch

1 inch = 25.4 millimeters

1 centimeter (cm) = .394 inch

1 inch = 2.54 centimeters

1 foot = 30.48 centimeters

1 foot = .305 meter

1 meter (m) = 39.37 inches, or 3.28 feet, or 1.09 yards

1 yard = .914 meter

1 kilometer (km) = 3,281 feet, or .62 mile

1 statute mile = 1.61 kilometers

Orienteering

For some people, being lost isn't enough. They have to make a game of it. If you're one of those, with good map-interpreting and compass skills, and if you think that running (or skiing or snow-shoeing in winter) through two to ten miles of backcountry sounds like fun, and if you have a competitive spirit—then you might like to try the sport of orienteering.

Orienteering races are set up so that partici-pants using maps, compasses, and cunning have to find a series of hidden control points in the pre-scribed order in the least amount of time. The courses are laid out over wooded terrain that is unfamiliar to all contestants. Upon starting, the runner is given a topographical map that is drawn to a large scale and small enough to be held in the hand. Maps can be standard USGS 1:24,000 scale topos, but are more often specially made topo maps at a 1:10,000 scale that are highly detailed and very up-to-date. The top of an orienteering map always represents magnetic (not the usual geographic) north, and vertical magnetic north lines are pre-drawn so there is no need to bother with declination. (These lines were the reason for the invention of the baseplate compass). As an additional aid, runners are also given a card with a brief written description of each control's location ("Control #3: At trail junction").

The locations of between five and fifteen orange-and-white control-point markers are circled on the map. The challenge is to quickly orient and interpret the map and get going toward the first control point as soon as possible. The object is to pick the fastest route, which is rarely a straight line. This is where map interpretation comes in. Is it faster to go over a hill, around it, partway up and follow a contour line, or use a level road that is longer but faster? You have to be able to visualize the best route and then follow it as fast and as accurately as possible. To do this you have to use all the tricks we've gone over in this book. Handrails, catch points, lines and points of refer-ence, aiming off, counting your pace to measure distance covered, and anything else you can think of. Compass work is often crude and fast, as taking bearings and plotting them is time-consuming. After the first control is found, you work your way through all the others. Whoever completes the course in the least time wins. But the winner is not always the fastest runner. The great equalizer in orienteering is that it is more often your wayfind-ing and mental ability rather than all-out speed that decides the winner.

There are also less competitive types of orien-teering activities offered by some clubs encourag-ing family participation. These laid-back events are for "wayfarers" or "map walkers," as they are called within the sport. For folks who like a chal-lenge but also want to stop and smell the flowers, watch the birds, or contemplate the meaning of magnetism or other esoterica as they amble along.

Orienteering started in Sweden in the 1920s and it still has a large following there. Competi-tions can attract thousands of runners to an event. The sport was introduced to the U.S. after World War II and now has a loyal, if somewhat more modest, following here. Those who get caught up in it can compete on the local, national, and inter-national level.

If this sounds like something you might want to try, contact the United States Orienteering Federation, Box 1444, Forest Park, GA 30051.

Satellite Navigation

The object of the preceding pages has been to answer one very simple question: "Where am I in relation to everything else?" As you've seen, getting that answer isn't always easy. And it's always been that way. Since before recorded time, all we've wanted is a magic box—press a button and, zap, it tells you where you are. A navigator's fantasy. Until now.

Right now that magic box exists in the form of a GPS (Global Positioning System) receiver. It's about the size of an overfed TV remote control, costs around $450 (in 1994, getting cheaper and smaller as time goes on), and can be bought from almost any up-scale outdoor or boating equipment supplier. They're rugged, waterproof, weigh about a pound, can be used in a boat, car, airplane, or snowmobile. Most need only a few AA batteries. They're very easy to use and can tell you:

- Your position by latitude and longitude, or Universal Transverse Mercator (UTM) coordinates.
- Altitude in feet or meters.
- Average speed.
- Direction to your destination.
- How far off course you are.
- Distance to your destination.
- How long it will take you to get to your destination.
- Estimated time of arrival.
- The path you've taken so you can follow it back, or retrace it in the future.

Like national parks and USGS topo maps, the wonderful GPS system is a result of our tax dollars (about $90 billion of them) at work—although they're really working for the military. Back in 1973, the U. S. Department of Defense wanted to provide continuous positioning and altitude information to U.S. military forces all over the globe. The goal was to encircle the world with twenty-one NavStar satellites (and three "spares") orbiting 12,000 miles above the earth.

Each satellite broadcasts its position in the heavens and the precise time (from an on-board atomic clock accurate to one second every 70,000 years). Your receiver notes the satellite's position and then measures the signal's time of travel from there to your receiver. That tells it how far away the satellite is from you. The distance is used as the radius of a circle with the satellite at the center, making a circular line of position. You are somewhere on this circle. To find out exactly where, the receiver gets two more circular lines of position from two other satellites. The point on the ground where the three circles cross is a fix—and your receiver translates that into latitude and longitude. Another circle from a fourth satellite gives the receiver your altitude. Most receivers have access to five or more satellites at a time, so you're pretty much covered, no matter where you go.

The potential accuracy of this system is astounding. But the military isn't ready to share its greatest accuracy with civilians. Satellites send out two types of signals. The Precision Positioning Service (PPS) is available only to U.S. military and their allies and is accurate to within 17.8 meters. This was successfully used during the Persian Gulf war of 1991. The Standard Positioning Service, which is available to everyone, is accurate to within one hundred meters. While you should not count on anything better than a hundred meters, users do experience times when accuracy is far better, often to twenty-five or thirty meters.

At this level of precision, the accuracy of even the finest cartography comes into question, which is why only the most up-to-date maps should be used. It is possible to use GPS without maps too, or in areas with no landmarks such as the desert or at sea. Fisherman return to a productive spot on the trackless ocean by entering a waypoint, the latitude and longitude of that location, into their receiver. To return they follow the magnetic compass course shown on the receiver, and watch their progress on the receiver's "steering" screen. Fancier receivers also have charts built into their memories. The map of your area comes up on the screen and a flashing point shows your position. So far this feature is available only for coastal regions, but will soon be expanded to cover more and more areas.

Sound great? Well, it is. But don't throw away your map and compass. It's still a gadget made up of microchips, circuit boards, and wire, and like a toaster or a TV set, it can go wrong. In addition, satellites can be a little off, or their signals may be affected by atmospheric conditions. Overall, the potential for errors within the GPS system is remarkably low. But if you are depending on this alone, that small probability can become a disaster when it happens. The prudent navigator should never rely on a single source for determining position, and always verifies results by other means.

Sources of Maps, Books, Compasses, and Videos

Maps

Each of the following federal agencies may carry different types of maps for the area you are interested in. To get the right maps when ordering, be specific about where you will be traveling, and the sort of maps you will need. It is best to call when ordering or requesting information. Not only is it faster, but you can often circumvent confusing bureaucratic double talk.

United States federal agencies:

Army Corps of Engineers, Department of
  Defense, Office of Public Affairs,
  Room 1101,
20 Massachusetts Ave. NW,
Washington, DC 20314.
(202) 272-0011.
*Covers navigable inland waterways, lakes, and
  rivers.*

Central Intelligence Agency (CIA), Public
  Affairs Office,
Washington, DC 20505.
(703) 351-2053.
*More than 100 maps of foreign countries avail-
  able to the public. Not all of use to wilderness
  explorers. Ask for "CIA Maps and Publications
  Released to the Public."*

Earth Resources Observation Systems
  (EROS), User Services Section,
U.S. Geological Survey, Sioux Falls,
  SD 57198.
(605) 594-6151.
*The clearinghouse for federal aerial photographs
  and space imagery.*

National Ocean Service (NOS),
Riverdale, MD 20737.
(301) 436-6990.
*Nautical charts for coastal waters, Great Lakes,
  and offshore. Aerial photos are also available.
  Charts can be found at most boating stores.
  For a complete description of symbols found on
  U.S. charts ask for "Chart No.1."*

National Park Service (NPS), Room 1013,
Washington, DC 20240.
(202) 208-4747.
Maps available for all national parks.

U.S. Forest Service (USFS), Public Affairs
  Office, 2nd Floor, Auditors Bldg.,
14th & Independence Ave. SW,
Washington, DC 20250.
(202) 205-1760.
Maps for all 155 national forests.

The Earth Science Information Center (ESIC) is the information and map sales branch of the U.S. Geological Survey (USGS). Call them at (800) USA-MAPS.

The USGS is the government's largest mapping agency, covering almost every inch of the U.S., its territories, most national parks, and Antarctica. Call, and they'll help you get the right maps. A good starting point is to get a free "Map Index" for the state you'll be traveling in (there's one for each state), and their brochure (also free) "Topographic Map Symbols." Also of interest is "How to Obtain Aerial Photographs." Maps can be ordered through ESIC, or they can direct you to a state agency or a local retail outlet.

Canadian government agencies:

Canada Map Office,
615 Booth St., Ottawa,
Ontario K1A 0E9.
(613) 952-7000.
*Source for the National Topographic Series of
  maps which cover all of Canada and its territories. Also distributes the Canadian National
  Parks Maps. Map indexes, price list, and
  brochures on request.*

Canadian Hydrographic Service, Department
  of Fisheries and Oceans,
1675 Russell Rd., Box 8080,
Ottawa, Ontario K1G 3H6.
(613) 998-4931.
*Nautical charts of coastal waters, Great Lakes,
  and major waterways.*

153

Other sources:

Check the Department of Tourism for the state or country that you will be traveling in.

Mail-order companies:

The following mail-order companies have extensive stocks of foreign and domestic maps. All are very helpful, and able to get you maps for some of the oddest places:

- Europe Map Service/OTD Ltd., 1 Pinewood Rd., Hopewell Junction, NY 12533. (914) 221-0208.
- ITMB Publishing Ltd., 736A Granville St., Vancouver, BC, V6Z 1G3, Canada. (604) 687-3320.
- Map Link, 25 E. Main St., Santa Barbara, CA 93101. (805) 965-4402.
- Omni Resources, 1004 S. Mebane St., Burlington, NC 27215. (800) 742-2677.
- The Map Store, 5821 Karric Square Dr., Dublin, OH 43017. (800) 332-7885.

To find a good map store near you, contact the International Map Dealers Association, Box 1789, Kankakee, IL 60901. (815) 939-4627.

Topo maps

The following sources provide topographical maps of the better-known parks and trails:

- Adirondack Mountain Club, RR 3, Box 3055, Lake George, NY 12845. (518) 668-4447. Maps for the Adirondack Reserve.
- Appalachian Mountain Club, 5 Joy St., Boston, MA 02108. (800) 262-4455. For the Northeast and the Appalachian mountain chain.
- Appalachian Trail Conference, Box 807, Harpers Ferry, WV 25425. (304) 535-6331. Covers the complete trail through 14 states.
- Buckeye Trail Association, Inc., Box 254, Worthington, OH 43085. Maps for the 1,200-mile trail.
- Clarkson Map Co., 1225 Delanglade St.,

Box 218, Kaukauna, WI 54130. (414) 766-300. The Canadian Boundary Waters of Minnesota, Michigan, and Wisconsin.

- Colorado Mountain Club, 2530 W. Alameda St., Denver, CO 80219. (303) 922-8315. For trails and wilderness areas.
- DeLorme Mapping Co., Box 298, Freeport, ME 04032. (207) 865-4171. Topo map atlases of many states. Scale 1:150,000.
- Earthwalk Press, 2239 Union St., Eureka, CA 95501. (701) 442-0503. Covers the parks and wilderness of the West and Hawaii.
- Finger Lakes Trail Conference, Inc., Box 18048, Rochester, NY 14618. Takes you through the 800-mile Finger Lake trail system.
- Florida Trail Association, Box 13708, Gainesville, FL 32604. (904) 378-8823. From South Florida to the panhandle.
- Green Mountain Club, RR 1, Box 650, Route 100, Waterbury Center, VT 05677. (802) 244-7037. Offers maps of the 265-mile Long Trail and others.
- Green Trails, Inc., Box 1932, Bothell, WA 98041. (206) 485-9144. For the Northwest.
- Tom Harrison Cartography, 333 Bellam Blvd., San Rafael, CA 94901. (415) 456-7940. Parks, forests, and wilderness areas of California.
- Kingfisher Maps, Inc., Box 1604, Seneca, SC 29679. (803) 882-5840. Waterproof topographic and bottom-contour maps for most lakes east of the Rockies.
- New England Cartographics, Box 369, Amherst, MA 01004. (413) 253-7415. Laminated or waterproof paper maps of the Northeast.
- Trails Illustrated, Box 3610, Evergreen, CO 80439. (303) 670-3457. Waterproof and tearproof maps of most national parks, plus recreational areas in Colorado and Utah. Include trail descriptions and visitor information. Up to date and excellent.

- University of Hawaii Press, University of Hawaii, Manoa, 2840 Kolowalu St., Honolulu, HI 96822. (808) 956-8255. Hawaii and Samoa.
- Wilderness Press, 2440 Bancroft Way, Berkeley, CA 94704. (510) 843-8080. Popular hiking areas in California.

Books

The Map Catalog, edited by Joel Makower, published by Tilden Press. An excellent resource book on maps, mapmaking, and map usage. Reviews all types of maps (not all of which are appropriate for wilderness use) and where to get them.

World Mapping Today, edited by R. B. Parry and C. R. Perkins, published by Butterworth. Provides graphic indexes for purchasing currently available maps, usually direct from government sources. International in scope. Need a topo of Swaziland? You'll find it here. General maps as well as topographical, environmental, geological, and others.

Emergency Navigation, by David Burch, International Marine Publishing Company, Camden, Maine. Its subtitle, *Pathfinding techniques for the inquisitive and prudent mariner,* is modest in its description. Good for sail or power craft on open waters.

Kayak Navigation, by David Burch, The Globe Pequot Press. For kayakers and canoeists when traveling along the coast. Simple, direct, and usable.

Compasses

- Brunton, 620 East Monroe Ave., Riverton, WY 82501. (307) 856-6559. Besides the usual variety, they also offer their patented floating emergency compass: a thin, small disk that floats on water.

- Silva Compasses, Box 966, Binghamton, NY 13902. (607) 779-2200. Very much geared to the sport of orienteering.

- Suunto USA, 2151 Las Palmas Dr., Carlsbad, CA 92009. (619) 931-6788, (800) 543-9124. High-quality, limited variety.

Videos

Everyone learns in a different way. If you feel the message comes across better when seen on TV, then try these videos:

ABC's of Compass and Map is a 25-minute video. The package includes an instruction pamphlet, workbook, the USGS map symbol guide, and a compass. From Brunton, 620 East Monroe Ave., Riverton, WY 82501. (307) 856-6559.

Finding Your Way in the Wild, 35 minutes, is available from Quality Video, Inc., 7399 Bush Lake Rd., Edina, MN 55439.

Travel Plan

Group Members:

1 Name: _____

   Address: _____

   _____

   Who to call in an emergency: _____

   _____

2 Name: _____

   Address: _____

   _____

   Who to call in an emergency: _____

   _____

3 Name: _____

   Address: _____

   _____

   Who to call in an emergency: _____

   _____

4 Name: _____

   Address: _____

   _____

   Who to call in an emergency: _____

   _____

   (Use back of sheet for additional members.): _____

   _____

List visually distinctive equipment: _____

_____

_____

_____

Description and location of car: _____

_____

_____

License number: _____

Date and time of departure from trailhead: _____

Name of trail to be taken: _____

Describe route (Note landmarks, rest/camp sites, objective, return route): _____

_____

_____

Possible alternate routes: _____

_____

_____

Estimated date and time of return: _____

Latest expected return date: _____

Person to call if overdue or in case of an emergency: _____

_____

INSTRUCTIONS: Photocopy and fill in above form. Leave completed form with responsible person. Contact this person as soon as you return!

INDEX